Industry and University

New Forms of Co-operation and Communication

ORGANISATION FOR ECONOMIC CO-OPERATION AND DEVELOPMENT

Pursuant to article 1 of the Convention signed in Paris on 14th December, 1960, and which came into force on 30th September, 1961, the Organisation for Economic Co-operation and Development (OECD) shall promote policies designed:

- to achieve the highest sustainable economic growth and employment and a rising standard of living in Member countries, while maintaining financial stability, and thus to contribute to the development of the world economy;
- to contribute to sound economic expansion in Member as well as non-member countries in the process of economic development; and
- to contribute to the expansion of world trade on a multilateral, non-discriminatory basis in accordance with international obligations.

The Signatories of the Convention on the OECD are Austria, Belgium, Canada, Denmark, France, the Federal Republic of Germany, Greece, Iceland, Ireland, Italy, Luxembourg, the Netherlands, Norway, Portugal, Spain, Sweden, Switzerland, Turkey, the United Kingdom and the United States. The following countries acceded subsequently to this Convention (the dates are those on which the instruments of accession were deposited): Japan (28th April, 1964), Finland (28th January, 1969), Australia (7th June, 1971) and New Zealand (29th May, 1973).

The Socialist Federal Republic of Yugoslavia takes part in certain work of the OECD (agreement of 28th October, 1961).

Publié en français sous le titre:
INDUSTRIE ET UNIVERSITÉ
NOUVELLES FORMES DE COOPÉRATION ET DE COMMUNICATION

© OECD, 1984
Application for permission to reproduce or translate all or part of this publication should be made to:
Director of Information, OECD
2, rue André-Pascal, 75775 PARIS CEDEX 16, France.

This report concentrates on new forms of co-operation and collaboration between industry and universities. Its aim is not to present a comprehensive inventory of the many types of traditional links between the two sectors, but rather to explore the current initiatives for closer interaction, the new motivations for collaboration on the part of both parties, novel approaches for individual countries, and problems and prospects for strengthening relations. To accomplish this, enquiries were conducted in fourteen Member countries*. The findings of these enquiries were extensively discussed, under the aegis of the Committee for Scientific and Technological Policy, by its Ad Hoc Group on University Research, in order to assess their promise and relevance for OECD countries as a whole.

Publication of this report has been authorised by the Secretary-General.

---

* Canada, Denmark, Finland, France, Germany, Ireland, Italy, Japan, Netherlands, Norway, Sweden, Switzerland, United Kingdom, and the United States.

Also available

THE FUTURE OF UNIVERSITY RESEARCH (March 1981)
(92 81 03 1) ISBN 92-64-12160-9 78 pages £3.00 US$7.50 F30.00

SCIENCES AND TECHNOLOGY POLICY FOR THE 1980s (November 1981)
(92 81 05 1) ISBN 92-64-12254-0 168 pages £6.20 US$13.75 F62.00

ASSESSING THE IMPACTS OF TECHNOLOGY ON SOCIETY (April 1983)
(93 83 01 1) ISBN 92-64-12409-8 80 pages £4.50 US$9.00 F45.00

Prices charged at the OECD Publications Office.

THE OECD CATALOGUE OF PUBLICATIONS and supplements will be sent free of charge
on request addressed either to OECD Publications Office,
2, rue André-Pascal, 75775 PARIS CEDEX 16, or to the OECD Sales Agent in your country.

TABLE OF CONTENTS

EXECUTIVE SUMMARY 7

INTRODUCTION. 11

I. HOW NETWORKS BEGIN. 17

    A. Networks Depend on the Level of Industrial
       Development 19
       1. From Informal to Formal Networks 20
       2. Universities and Regional Development. 21
       3. University/Industry Relations in Less
          Industrialised Countries 24

    B. Networks Depend on the Scale and
       Branch of Industry. 25
       1. Large Firms in High Technologies 26
       2. Large Firms in Traditional Sectors 27
       3. Small and Medium Size Firms in
          High Technologies. 27
       4. Small and Medium Size Firms in
          Traditional Sectors. 29

II. HOW NETWORKS FUNCTION. 34

    A. Promotion of Long-Term Linkages Between
       Universities and Industry 34
       1. Incentives and Deregulation. 34
       2. Science Parks. 35
       3. University-Originated Firms. 36
       4. Long-Term Industry-University Partnerships 38

    B. Promotion of Special Areas of Science
       and Technology 41
       1. Basic Technologies for New Industries (Japan). . . . 41
       2. The SERC Directorate Programmes (UK) 42
       3. Special Programmes 43
       4. Co-operative Schemes 44

    C. Development of Liaison Systems. 47
       1. Transfer Points. 48
       2. Regional Brokers 49
       3. Industrial Register. 49
       4. Evolution of the Role of University
          Liaison Systems. 49
       5. Industrial Research Education Programme. 50

    D. From Knowledge to Products. 51
        1. The Swiss Impulse Programme. 53
        2. McGill University Value-Engineering Workshop 53
        3. The German Pilot Programme for New Technology-
           oriented Firms 54

CONCLUSIONS 56
    A. The Perequisites for Success. 56
    B. Universities and Innovation 60
    C. Strengthening the Socio-Technical Community 63

NOTES AND REFERENCES. 66

INDEX 67

EXECUTIVE SUMMARY

This report emphasizes the importance of informal networks between individuals in universities and industry which create the necessary basis for co-operation between the industrial and academic worlds on specific projects, and which may lead to continuing and broader collaboration once they are established. Thus, it attempts to identify the many factors which lead to the creation of networks and which subsequently facilitate or impede their evolution. From these considerations, a number of conclusions and proposals are drawn for review by government, university and industry. These fall essentially into three broad categories.

Conditions for Successful Co-operation

On the side of higher education (which includes universities as well as many other types of establishments), it is stressed that excellence in research is a prerequisite for fruitful collaboration with industry. This does not preclude, however, the need for a diversity of scientific work which should ideally cover a broad scope of activities ranging from basic research through strategic and targetted research projects to the provision of consultative services.

Industry, on the other hand, cannot expect to draw the full benefits offered by academic research unless it formulates its own problems and goals in terms of the opportunities offered by contemporary science and technology. This may prove difficult for certain types of industries, in particular small and medium size firms, and may require special assistance from outside including especially the scientific community itself.

The development of industry-university relations depends to an enormous extent on individual and institutional initiatives, mostly of an informal nature. This requires an environment which encourages relations between the two sectors, as well as a high level of institutional flexibility to pursue different approaches and modes of co-operation. In many Member countries regulations which constrain university scientists in their relationships with non-academic bodies constitute serious obstacles. To overcome these, incentives should be established to promote various forms of joint efforts by industry and universities in research, education and retraining. Lines of communication, through liaison offices, as well as mobility of personnel should be multiplied.

Universities and Innovation

Although safeguards may be required to prevent distortions in the university's basic functions, collaboration with industry can help to achieve more direct and rapid application of research results. Universities can provide a breeding ground for new companies, assist existing firms, collaborate on a continuing basis with high technology firms, and develop new forms of co-operation with mature industries.

Assistance to infant industrial firms in high technology areas may include:

-- "incubator factories" schemes designed by some universities to assist new firms;

-- provision of technical assistance for product development by universities;

-- provision by universities of venture capital required by colleagues who found new firms.

Many efforts to promote growth of high technology industries have focused on small and medium size firms. This may involve, in particular, the participation of university scientists in providing:

-- quality control, evaluation and testing services;

-- scientific and information services.

The mismatch between the general capabilities of universities and the highly specific needs of small firms limit the possibilities for direct collaboration. Yet, universities have occasionally succeeded in initiating co-operation with small firms through various mechanisms:

-- the placement of graduate students in an industrial environment and their involvement in the solution of industrial problems;

-- offering statutory opportunities to academic personnel so that they become more available as consultants and can be remunerated for these services;

-- developing relations with "industrial consortia", various intermediary and collective research bodies.

One of the salient features of the connections between large, science-based companies and universities is their long-term aspect, potential for continuity, and variety. To avoid arrangements which could disrupt other university functions or prove inimical to university concerns, it may be advisable to spell out a code of proper conduct in this area. It may also be useful to:

-- determine areas where public funds can play a "seeding function" through the provision of advanced facilities and equipment;

-- encourage public establishments to participate in industry/university co-operative arrangements.

It is often difficult to initiate linkages between "old" industries and traditional universities:

-- on the industrial side, management should seriously consider the setting up of university liaison services to initiate contacts with university groups;

-- the inclusion of engineering education and technological research on campus may generate new prospects for industrial contacts in traditional establishments of higher education;

-- the development of industrial liaison programmes may start from the university side, with efforts to increase informal contacts (through social occasions, seminars, etc.) with industry.

Strengthening the Socio-Technical Community

The importance of individual initiative in the formation and development of networks with industrial and academic participants cannot be underestimated. It must also be noted that these networks often begin in a regional development context. For this reason, one major goal of long-term policies for strengthening university-industry relations will be the creation or extension of socio-technical communities which provide opportunities for people with different backgrounds (large high-technology firms, mature industries, small firms, regional and national governments, traditional as well as new universities, scientists of all disciplines) to become personally acquainted, to understand their respective motivations, interests and constraints, and to explore the possibilities and mutual benefits offered by co-operation.

*

*   *

In the last decade, industry-university relations have undergone major shifts and changes. Traditional approaches have turned out to be insufficient in the face of rising expectations stimulated by intense international competition. Although industry still expects the universities to focus their primary efforts on the training (and re-training) of scientists and engineers, academic research is increasingly seen as offering specific opportunities which call for co-operation. Long-term national and international "megabuck" research deals, close integration of industrial and university teams, new demands for university initiatives in the diffusion and application of research results, increasing involvement of academic scientists and engineers of all disciplines in regional development -- are some of the main new features of present trends.

Attempts at forceful co-ordination and control could be counter-productive. But governments can facilitate and encourage these trends, for example, by adjustment of legal and regulatory constraints, provision of adequate incentives to all parties, development of national programmes to pull together scattered efforts. They can help in the creation of a milieu where initiatives multiply and bear fruit.

Governments also have a decisive responsibility in safeguarding the fundamental functions of universities in the creation of basic knowledge and the training of new generations of highly skilled professionals and scholars.

The report has been prepared by Stuart Blume, Georges Ferné and Michael Gibbons under the direction of Georges Ferné. A very large number of government, university and industrial officials have, however, participated in the different stages of enquiries and discussions and have provided the substance of the reflections which had to be presented below in a concise form. Although it would be impossible to acknowledge each individual by name, their contributions have been essential.

INTRODUCTION

Scientific and technological information and know-how play a key role in the process of technological innovation and <u>a fortiori</u> in economic growth. Although the output of innovative activity is typically a new product or process technology, the activity itself, it is now understood, is primarily about the selection and control of information. The innovation process is uncertain precisely because, when the relevant information is still unidentified, firms are often required to look widely in attempting to find competitive solutions to their myriad technical problems. During this process, management begins to review their recruitment policies and to broaden, generally, the information resources available to it.

From this perspective, technological innovation could almost be described as the attempt to institutionalise the search for new types of information within the business enterprises that collectively make up "industry". One of the most potent sources of such information lie distributed in the network of higher education institutions [1]. As a consequence, not only are universities and polytechnics implicated in the essence of innovation but their involvement is likely to become more intense when industry is faced with major changes to its basic technologies; that is, during times of pronounced structural change.

There is a mass of economic and other evidence now available to suggest that the economic downturn which began in the early 1970s and subsequently developed into the deepest recession since the thirties had its root cause less in the series of oil price rises which began in 1973 and more in the failure to prevent accelerating inflation within OECD countries and in the relative and absolute declines in the productivity of manufacturing industry. More fundamentally, it is becoming increasingly clear that these declining productivity levels reflected, in part, the exhaustion of the technical possibilities of certain long-standing methods of production, principally in motor vehicles, synthetic fibres and electronics. It is because of this that throughout the 1970s and into the 1980s, industry has been faced with the consequences of structural change; that is, with the need to transform the basis of its productive activities by introducing new technology. One upshot of this has been a renewed interest on the part of many industrial firms, large and small, in the research activities of the higher education sector. This burgeoning interest, which is founded partly on need, is currently both informal and experimental and is establishing a number of new forms of collaboration and communication.

To a large extent, the industrial interest has been reciprocated by the higher education sector. This sector is, in most Member countries, an extremely expensive social overhead, financed more or less directly from the wealth-creating activities of industry. The current wave of recession has been much longer and deeper than many expected and the environment of declining public resources established in its wake has affected institutions of higher education of many Member countries profoundly. Not only has the higher education sector in most Member countries ceased to grow over the past decade but cut-backs, early retirements and in some cases redundancies have induced the universities to examine their functions afresh. Many have concluded that if research is to continue, traditional governmental sources of finance for research will have to be augmented by industry. However, as is well known, industry's research requirements are different from those of the university and mutual accommodation still remains a challenge at a time when both sets of institutions face major problems.

Diversity

In a regime of greater than average structural change, when trying to introduce new technology, industry is often being forced to experiment with new forms of collaboration with the universities. Because of the inter-dependence of industrial technologies, these initiatives cover a wide range of industries and involve firms of different sizes utilising technologies with very different potentials for development. Given the experimental nature of these initiatives, judgements about success or failure of a particular form of collaboration must be made in relation to what is expected on the one hand and what is possible, on the other. And, in any case, their very nature is related to the concrete situation of a particular country, its stage of industrial development, its scale of industrial activity and the stage of development of its research system.

Balance of Functions

The primary function of the institutions of higher education is teaching and (in the case of the universities) research. It is generally agreed that these functions are fundamental and ought not to be compromised. This report, then, reflects a predominant view that can in particular be identified in a series of OECD reports; most recently in The Future of University Research (2). However, these fundamental functions can be supplemented in a variety of ways and universities should learn to do some things better than they do at present. The principal concern is that an excessive increase in new functions, beyond those of teaching and research, by these institutions will result in a kind of "functional overload" with the probable result that even the prime functions will be performed inadequately -- the more so if resources do not grow while external demands become more pressing.

Looking for the unquantifiable

The message which emerges from this is clear but it is not simple: the complexity of new forms of university/industry relations reflect the variations in types of industries and capacities, values and interests of higher education institutions. This can be illustrated with respect to funding statistics, the growth patterns of university/industry relations and the range of goals to be achieved by schemes aimed at promoting these relations.

For the most part, the statistics relating to industry/university relations focus on the financial contribution of industry to the funding of research performed in universities and are often based on gross estimates. Efforts are underway to attain more precision in evaluating this particular flow of funding. In any case, the general picture which emerges from an overview of the share of R&D expenditures in higher education financed by industry illustrates the broad diversity of situations of funding ranging from $488 000 in Ireland to close to $ 200 million in the United States. More revealing perhaps, the share of R&D expenditures in higher education financed by the business enterprise sector ranged from 0.2 per cent in Canada in 1979, to close to 12 per cent in Switzerland. Seven countries only -- France, Germany, Ireland, the Netherlands, Switzerland, the United Kingdom and the United States -- had passed the 2 per cent mark. Looking at the actual trend in this area in the past decade it became quite obvious that Member countries have followed very different paths. Growth has been very rapid, for example, in France and Switzerland where industrial funding has more than quadrupled in the decade. The level of spending has been relatively steady in the United States and Japan. It has actually declined in the United Kingdom between 1973 and 1977 but seems to have started growing again. In fact several countries underwent a slow-down or a decline in the growth of this type of funding in the middle of the decade.

One could certainly draw the conclusion that several countries have undergone major changes in the pattern of relations between higher education and industry in research. Some countries, like France, have seen this network of relations improve while others have basically pursued a long trend of growth; while still others have witnessed a certain loosening, if not a decline, in the established pattern of relations. These indications must, however, be interpreted with a great deal of prudence. It is well known that a large share of the financial flow from industry to universities is not accounted for officially and formally in national statistics: many contacts, when they develop, establish themselves between particular firms and particular members of the university community and thus will not always appear as such in any account of the research funding within a particular academic institution. More importantly, much of the collaboration does not necessarily constitute actual funding of research. The arrangements which may be made between university scientists and industry take many forms: equipment may be made available to scientists without an actual transfer of funds; funding may be focused on fellowships and scholarships for promising students and will not necessarily be accounted for as a contribution to research; contacts may simply involve a personal relationship between a university professor and researchers in industry. The fact that all these types of exchanges and relations do not involve transfer of monies does not necessarily mean that they are of less importance or significance than others. In fact, they may, on the whole, play a much more crucial role at present than the actual funding by industry of research performed in universities.

Industry/university relations are multi-purpose ones, directed to educational goals as well as research targets, and are highly complex and diversified. It has occasionally been argued that attempts at quantifying some of these relations -- for example, personal and informal relationships between university professors and industry such as those that are frequent in Japan -- would in themselves have an impact which is not necessarily desirable.

Is every case unique?

Two problems emerge from this complexity: the difficulty of conveying the typical development of a new form of collaboration and the difficulty in assessing the effectiveness of the particular case. With regard to the former, the case of Rennsselaer Polytechnic Institute in the United States provides an excellent example of the "on-going" or open-ended nature of university/industry relations. It could be said that this example provides an "ideal type" of what was being looked for throughout the study.

Rennsselaer Polytechnic Institute (USA)

"Today, one of our most successful relationships with industry is in computer graphics -- in computer-aided design. This relationship is all encompassing, it involves an affiliated program with many companies; specific research and problem solving arrangements with individual firms; continuing education and training programs, both broadly based and specifically tailored for a company's needs; consulting by faculty members and an exchange wherein people from industry serve as adjunct faculty in our institution. It also involves the payment of fees by industry, and gifts or loans of equipment and software. Above all, it involves an exchange of ideas and knowledge that is beneficial to both partners.

"Today, we can count more than 100 separate arrangements and agreements with industry in this program alone.

"But we did not start out with industry relations in mind. In fact, our computer graphics effort had its genesis about seven years ago in a desire to improve undergraduate engineering education. We were concerned about the loss of all hands on experience in the curriculum such as drafting, surveying, and shop courses -- and searched for the modern equivalent of these. The answer was in the then emerging new tool of the engineer -- the interactive computer graphics terminal. We set up a classroom of 36 terminals, driven by two mini computers, and developed demonstration programs for most of our undergraduate engineering courses. Soon 2 700 students, our entire undergraduate engineering enrollment, passed through that classroom every year.

"Next came graduate education and research. Graduate students were first involved in developing the computer programs for undergraduate teaching demonstrations. From this, they and their faculty saw opportunities for fundamental research, both in the development of graphics techniques, and in their applications. Physically, this research is conducted in the same laboratory complex that includes the undergraduate classroom, thus assuring linkages between graduate and undergraduate education.

"All of this happened in a period when industry recognised computer-aided design as a fundamental tool in its quest for improved quality and increased productivity. The all-pervasive ties with industry, which I described, thus were a natural outcome of our

> educational program -- a program that clearly had its own intrinsic academic value, and that value is still maintained today."
>
> The President of RPI

One difficulty which arises in considering this example lies in the fact that although it is a good example of a success story it provides little guidance in identifying failures on other cases. But how does one measure success in this area? It would certainly seem vital to acquire a better understanding of the factors which make a project, once launched jointly by a university team and a firm, a successful one. Most enquiries and studies, up to now, have focused on the live, rather than the dead efforts. Future attempts at clarifying the nature of the relationship at stake, and the conditions for success, should certainly also focus on the failures. For the time being, however, the data on which one could base such an evaluation remain very patchy. In addition, there are obvious difficulties in evaluating "success" when it is largely a matter of perspective.

In France, the academic institutions in the Languedoc, a relatively under-industrialised region of France, are in receipt of large and growing research funds. But almost all contractual work is done on behalf of national firms. There are virtually no links with local industry. As a consequence, those responsible for the economic development of the region view the situation with disquiet. That different views may be taken, may be readily illustrated by the Centre for Cold Ocean Resources and Engineering "C-CORE" of Memorial University, Newfoundland, Canada. The distinction between the two situations is, of course, that C-CORE is judged in terms of its national role, while in the Languedoc precisely this and the lack of a regional role is seen as a cause for anxiety. In such areas, the position of the academic institutions is an ambiguous one which can only be resolved by answering the question "what is expected of the universities here?".

> "C-CORE", Newfoundland (Canada)
>
> Newfoundland itself is a relatively under-developed part of Canada, geographically remote from Canada's main development corridor which roughly follows the St. Lawrence river, between Montreal and the Great Lakes. C-CORE is engaged in engineering research designed to assist in the safe and orderly development and utilisation of Canada's ocean resources. Its research is deliberately intended to focus on problems of national interest and of long-term interest to industry and government. The Centre has established some 30 industrial associations, including many of Canada's largest petroleum companies. Since its establishment, in 1975, C-CORE has done with distinction just what it was set up to do, even though the operative university-industry networks do not, in the main, involve local industry.

*

* *

The organisation of this report is to a large extent determined by the method used in gathering information. Essentially, it presents an analysis of the information contained in fourteen country reports (3). Although each case study stands on its own, it was felt to be important in presenting the conclusions to deal with the complexity that is often the concomitant of individuality. Chapter I selects from the case study data the variety of types of networks of collaboration operative in different countries. In particular, networks are analysed in relation to industrial development, in relation to the scale of industrial activity and in relation to the organisation of higher education in individual countries. In Chapter II, new forms of university-industry relations are categorised by the function that they are intended to fulfill: long-term linkages; promotion of special areas of science and technology; and the development of liaison systems.

I. HOW NETWORKS BEGIN

A set of informal university/industry relations operates in all countries more or less extensively and effectively. In some cases, these are still at an early stage; in others the universities during the last 10 to 15 years have, in attempting to improve the efficiency and scope of these relationships, merely formalised them. Perhaps more as a consequence of the major new technologies than anything else, new informal networks are emerging and in many countries there are attempts by government and industry to spur on the development of these relationships so as to maximise the likelihood of being able to "cash-in" on the fruit of biotechnology, information technology, industrial robotics, etc.

Yet, it is often difficult to characterise these networks and to assess their strengths and weaknesses. For example, in different contexts, the expectations vested in these relationships are far from clear. What contributions are the universities expected to make to industrial innovation?

Institutions of higher education -- from universities to polytechnics -- may be new or old, traditional or technological, aimed broadly at advancing science in an international context or, more narrowly, at meeting the needs of the local community. Although a function of this system certainly is the performance of basic, predominantly long-term research, this commitment may vary according to the type of establishment concerned. It remains, however, that in all cases quality remains a central aspiration. In Japan and the United States, for example, despite all the concern about research oriented to national needs, there is a real effort to ensure that excellence in research is maintained and even strengthened. All universities -- even those which are clearly expected to respond to regional demands -- will also be expected to strive for national and even international scientific recognition. The duality of purposes may not be as drastic as it would seem: there is some evidence that there is a close connexion between quality of education and research in a given institution, and the level of industrial support for research by contract.

In all industrialised countries, most universities argue, plausibly, that their level of industrial financing for research is more closely related to their acknowledged excellence than to any other single factor. This same point was made implicitly earlier when it was noted that close links frequently exist between major R&D oriented firms and the stronger institutions of higher education. There can be little doubt that the strongest firms "look for an equal partner". However, for some such firms, and in some countries, the problem is that there are no really "equal" partners. For example, scientists in the German firm Siemens are regarded as members of the international scientific community in various areas and, in these, their resources far exceed those which universities could reasonably expect to invest if they genuinely wanted to follow the "equal partner" option. Firms in this situation often maintain that the principal function of the university is to train highly qualified manpower and, understandably, their links with universities reflect this interest. Further, the growth of science parks and such phenomena as Route 128, Silicon Gulch and Silicon Glen are not conspicuously successful without the existence of and support from major research universities. It is perhaps no accident that science parks have flourished around universities such as MIT, Stanford (United States), Cambridge (United Kingdom) and Grenoble (France) and that these institutions serve as breeding grounds for the entrepreneurs who establish high technology spin-off firms in the vicinity of them.

It may be that it will be necessary to consider the institutions of higher education more closely according to the functions they are expected to perform in relation to industry. For example, some universities might become expert in dealing with the problems of a given set of small and medium sized firms. Many universities in the OECD area already seem to be acquiring certain specialities: for example, in Finland in relation to regional development and, in France, by developing specific roles, as in the cases of the Université Louis Pasteur (Strasbourg) and the Université de Haute Alsace (Mulhouse), where the latter has oriented its research activities to serve regional industries to a larger extent than the former which clearly has a national, even international, scope of activities.

Even more spectacular specialisation has occurred when, as in many OECD countries, the technological disciplines have become the sole province of the technological universities. Where this distinction is well entrenched, there is much evidence to indicate that these institutions have qualitatively different links with industry. For example, although Siemens in Germany has a variety of research contract links to the German university system it is to the technological university in Munich that Siemens has looked to for its employees: it has not been exceptional to see almost entire classes of the Electronics Department recruited by Siemens.

The technical universities and polytechnics have come to fulfil this role for obvious reasons. Of course, it is partly their function -- what they were set up to do in the first place -- and partly, it is a matter of the subjects taught and the research interests of the staff; and the fact that industry recruits engineers and therefore has a more direct interest in what is being taught and worked on than might be expected with respect to a traditional university. But while these elements no doubt play a part in the formation of their distinctive relations with industry, there is another, perhaps more significant, fact involved. It is hard to escape the conclusion, most obvious in the technical universities, that the staff there operate in a different culture and are motivated by different commitments than those which appear, at least on the surface, at the traditional universities. Thus, one cannot ignore the fact that technological universities such as Chalmers in Sweden or Compiègne in France, for example, are institutions that have successfully differentiated their role from that of the traditional universities and that, rather than continually trying to copy the larger more prestigious traditional universities, they have established another culture and ethos to the extent that it is not too surprising to hear that "it would feel wrong to do basic, useless, research in Chalmers".

The significance of this development is difficult to overstate. In many countries, where new institutions of higher education were established during the 1960s with the exclusive job of providing technical excellence in specific areas or problem-solving support for the local as opposed to the national community, there has been a conspicuous lack of success in establishing such an alternative culture. Instead, the values of the traditional institution of higher education (which of course provided the first generation of personnel for new institutions) have been predominant to such an extent that, in the end, they have become the model to be followed. The result, of course, has been profoundly disappointing because, not only has the technical ethos failed to emerge but the attempt at copying the traditional universities has not been a notable success either. As a result these new institutions have the worst of both worlds; they attract neither the interest of the national research councils nor the support of industry. Chalmers University and the Université technologique de Compiègne give clear examples of what is possible, though, as they make clear, such a "profound transformation of values cannot take place quickly". This is a real problem and it is far from clear that it will be solved by further developments in bureaucratic styles of management which seem to be springing up in so many institutions. However, SINTEF in Norway shows what can be done in the way of grafting on to an existing institution an organisation which embodies different values and structures from the originating ones. While such grafting may lead to a gradual shift of values and evolution of structures, such change cannot be rapid and it is very much an open question whether this pace of change will be sufficient to the needs of industrial societies in the 1990s.

It is tempting to be defeatist on the possibilities of major institutional change and to follow the route, say, of Finland or Japan or the Netherlands and develop new institutions to meet specific needs. It is true that, for example, Kuopio and Oulu in Finland, and perhaps Twente in the Netherlands, have succeeded in developing new functions and, as a consequence, a distinct network of relationship with industry. But it is not clear why they have been successful. For example, in the case of Finland, Kuopio and Oulu were motivated, on the positive side, by a desire to bring traditional university skills to bear on regional problems and organise themselves accordingly. The university/industry networks which have resulted follow directly from this prior commitment to regional development.

Still, there can be little doubt that disciplinary structures tend to be more formally established in traditional universities and that it is often more difficult -- and therefore much slower -- to accommodate multidisciplinary research or promote large-scale project work that involves co-operation across departmental boundaries.

A. NETWORKS DEPEND ON THE LEVEL OF INDUSTRIAL DEVELOPMENT

Collaboration and communication between industry and the academic community usually begin very informally and are characterised by person-to-person contacts. From this base, they may gradually become more and more formal, leading eventually to contracts and/or other forms of linkages. What is essential is to identify the various factors (social, institutional, legal, attitudinal, etc.) which will stimulate this type of evolution.

1. From Informal to Formal Networks

Among OECD countries there are a number in which university/industry relations have long been viewed as outstanding, providing a model for others to emulate. Switzerland is one such country. Moreover, it is one in which intimate and effective relations have seemingly owed little or nothing to governmental initiative: federal government policy has been highly non-interventionist, and the Swiss example is pre-eminently one of the efficacy of informal relations. Unusually close relations have developed, over a long period, based essentially on common memberships, clubs, shared educational experiences, linking the nation's economic and scientific leaders and thus constituting what could be called a genuine "socio-technical community". Such links have been particularly close in binding together the most powerful among the firms and the educational institutions (notably the two Federal Institutes of Technology).

In the case of the Federal Institute of Technology (Zurich -- ETH), links have become highly institutionalised, and involve participation of industry on the boards responsible for up-dating curricula and for selecting professors; recruitment of industrialists as permanent lecturers and full-time professors; subsidisation by industry of post-graduate research and assistant posts (250 at present); liberal allocation of consultancy contracts to academics; and the provision of research "mandates" (broadly defined research of a fundamental or strategic character financed by industry).

Firms enjoying good links with academic institutions perceive that they must keep their partners in touch with their own research activities and try to develop a true complementarity of work. It is in this way that relations between academic institutions and firms, notably in the fields of mechanical engineering, chemicals and pharmaceuticals, achieved an effectiveness that came widely to be admired (4). It should be stressed that industrial links with universities in Switzerland, where they are successful, are based upon a sense of mutual respect, a "give and take among equals", which is at the root of a relationship which could not have developed without it -- that is, without the crucial element of person-to-person familiarity and confidence.

However, the adequacy of existing relations is increasingly being called into question. In Switzerland, the dramatic decline of the watchmaking industry, under the impact of new technology adopted far more rapidly by firms elsewhere, provided a pronounced shock when it underlined the difficulty of industry in keeping up with the sources of technological progress and anticipating major changes. It has come to be seen that existing networks do not suffice to enable Swiss industry in general to take advantage of emerging technological opportunities. The need for new approaches by government authorities, industry and universities has increasingly been felt. The Federal Institute of Technology (Zurich) has established a contract research organisation, as has the University of Geneva. The Federal Institute of Technology (Lausanne) has established a Prospective Research Centre to co-ordinate the activities of the various institutes and their relations with the economic sector. The Centre has a somewhat broader and, as its name suggests, more "prospective" task in relation to links with industry than are commonly vested in Industrial Liaison Officers. A number of initiatives have been taken in order to provide technical assistance to small firms, for example the Consultancy Office for Technical Innovation established by the Chambers of Commerce of Berne and Soleure.

In other countries, and of course even more so in those which have never been viewed as providing "models" for industry-university relations, similar concerns are manifest. Furthermore attention has also turned to the small and medium sized firms which dominate the industrial structure of many countries. In Japan, for example, present dissatisfaction with existing relationships reflects to some extent growing concern with the importance and problems of small and medium sized firms. But in the case of Japan there is another, unique, circumstance. This is the relatively recent, but widespread, recognition that the leadership which the country has achieved in many of the most vital areas of new technology means that past strategies of importing basic knowledge for industrial use are no longer available. Japan will have to create the knowledge upon which its industrial future depends by itself.

Thus, in seeking to extend university/industry relations more broadly, a range of new initiatives is being discussed and implemented in almost all Member countries. At a certain level of industrial development, a country is bound to confront one of three basic questions. Either, like Switzerland, what more should be done on the basis of existing informal and formal networks? Or, like Japan, how can existing informal relations lead to more established and systematic arrangements? Or, like the United Kingdom, how could one create a "socio-technical community" through the development of the basic informal relationships which might eventually turn into more formal links?

In the United Kingdom the view has long been that academics and industrialists live in different worlds, with little sense of each others needs, and little of the mutual respect noted in the case of Switzerland. Over the years the matter has been a major preoccupation of the Science and Technology Agencies of government, of the Research Councils, and of the Confederation of British Industry. Post-war years have seen countless initiatives designed to put the universities more effectively at the service of industry. The designation of a number of Universities of Technology in the 1960s, and later of a number of Polytechnics, and the setting-up of a number of university-industry liaison units by the Ministry of Technology, were in part an attempt to establish a distinctive segment of higher education better tuned to the needs of industry for manpower and research than seemed to be the case with existing universities. In recent years the Science and Engineering Research Council, in particular, has sought through its postgraduate training programmes to provide for the needs of industry for research manpower, and through the establishment of priorities (notably in engineering) to orient university research more to industrial problems. Partly at the initiative of universities themselves there has been a rapid diffusion of industrial liaison offices and units; a number of universities have established commercial companies; and a variety of other new forms of networks have begun to be developed (by the Technological Universities -- such as Aston and Salford -- in particular). Though traditions seem to be a major barrier in the United Kingdom it is far from clear whether relationships in the past have actually been as ineffective as is widely believed. Nevertheless, the fact is that the visible structure of relations in the United Kingdom, unlike Switzerland or Japan, is largely based upon identifiable initiatives taken over a long period.

2. Universities and Regional Development

Within many of the more industrialised Member countries there exist significantly less industrialised regions whose social and economic development has for some years been a matter of concern. In many cases, the recent past has led to a growing awareness of the potential role of research generally, and of institutions of higher education particularly, in bringing about the desired objectives of regional policies.

In Finland, France, Norway and Sweden, amongst others, regional policy has for some two decades been a major factor in the formulation of national higher education and research policies. Thus it was not uncommon in the 1960s, in planning for the expansion of numbers in higher education which took place throughout the OECD area at that time, deliberately to locate new institutions in less developed regions. These tended to be regions of largely rural activity, principally engaged in agriculture, fisheries, forestry.

Experience suggests that under certain conditions universities can play a significant role in relation to regional economic development. What above all seems necessary is a strong sense of regional identity, a wide identification with the specific problems and needs of the region, supported by a powerful regional impetus to change things. This impetus may derive from the regionalisation of central government policy, or it may derive from the determined efforts of individual regional authorities. It also seems clear that specific individuals, men of influence actively involved in a number of interlocking advisory and decision-making bodies, can play a major catalytic role in effectively bringing this regional consciousness to bear.

Finland, Norway and France provide examples of how university/industry relations can work effectively to the benefit of regions. The Finnish and Norwegian examples show above all the impact of new institutions of higher education seeking new roles in a regional perspective; the French example shows how initiatives can effectively be taken to establish new connexions between an established higher education system and its economic environment.

Characteristic of the Northern and Eastern regions of Finland are the attempts made by universities newly established (mostly in the 1960s) actively to seek to develop roles appropriate to their localities. Unencumbered by inherited notions of "what a university is supposed to be", those of Oulu, Kuopio, Joensuu, etc., have sought to define their new roles through negotiation and practice. The result is, in many ways, original and the work of these universities has certain unique features. For example:

-- numbers of university departments sought <u>ab initio</u> to orient their whole research effort around locally relevant problems (for example geography, local flora and fauna of economic importance);

-- the initial focus has often been on infrastuctural problems and development (e.g. working with local communities on formulation of development plans, or planning transportation or housing or energy supply) rather than on generating technical solutions for industry. This work may involve departments of economics, geography, or sociology as well as science and engineering;

-- a holistic approach which has been adopted in places is a unique development worthy of particular consideration. In one university, for instance, a department of zoology addresses its research and its educational work to the whole range of problems significant to the local fishing industry, from fish genetics and physiology to processing and marketing of fish products and to sociological studies of fishing communities. Elsewhere in Finland there are examples of such holistic projects bringing in the whole range of university expertise in a concerted attack on the multiple problems of a firm or industry.

A conscious regional development policy has also been pursued by Norway during more than 30 years: initiated as a special development plan for North Norway in 1952, it was subsequently extended to the country as a whole and is administered by the Regional Development Fund. Although the creation of new industry in the regions was emphasized at the outset, the efforts developed into a more comprehensive programme, i.e. with a view to securing equal access to social services, educational and cultural activities. The creation of the new University of Tromsø in 1968 may be viewed as a result of the regional development policy, and research carried out at this university is supposed to pay due regard to regional problems in North Norway.

Since then, a number of developments have occurred across the country:

-- the increasing number of young people seeking higher education led from 1969 to 1984 to the creation of 13 regional colleges, linked to particular counties; although the original intention was that these colleges should only provide shorter term education of an occupational kind, the teaching staffs soon pressed to embark upon research, mainly of applied character related to local problems;

-- a further development was initiated in the county of Røgaland in 1973 with the creation of an independent research foundation, Røgaland Research, closely attached to Røgaland Regional College; the North Sea Oil operations West of Stavanger played an important role in the establishment of the Foundation, which also established good contact with local industry and county and municipal authorities;

-- the example of Røgaland has led in several other counties to the establishment of similar institutions, Nordland Research, More Research, Agder Research, etc., linked to the regional colleges;

-- a similar foundation is to be established by the University of Tromsø in collaboration with the county authorities in North Norway, local industry and banking;

-- the Norwegian school of Economics and Business Administration in Bergen has recently re-organised its Center for Applied Research into an independent research foundation patterned on the SINTEF-model;

-- there is also growing interest in the creation of science parks, and Tromsø and other regions might follow the example set in this respect by the Oslo area.

The Science Policy Council for Norway (previously the Central Committee for Norwegian Research) has welcomed these developments in its report No. 6 of 1982, stressing also the important role the regional colleges may play in the dissemination of research results. Efforts in this direction have been initiated by the regional college' board and local authorities in the county of Telemark.

The Finnish and Norwegian examples show how higher education institutions (and perhaps especially new universities, because they tend to be more flexible than others) can assist in the articulation and achievement of regional socio-economic goals. Their effectiveness in drawing upon the broad range of expertise available within them has been a consequence of their aspiration for regional acceptance and legitimacy.

The case of France is different and does not depend upon new universities having sought to develop new goals. Rather, it has been a matter of taking specific initiatives to bring into being better connexions between established academic institutions and the industrial structure surrounding them. However here too success has depended upon (in some areas) deeply rooted regional consciousness and the growing importance of regionalism in policy. Bodies such as Regional Chambers of Commerce and regional planning bodies have often provided crucial forums in which key individuals have been able to operate. So too did the regional meetings which took place in preparation for the "Colloque national" on science and technology which took place in January 1982 at the initiative of the government. Beyond this, the regionalisation of certain key funding and information organisations has been of crucial significance. For example, the Centre national de la recherche scientifique (CNRS) has recently established a network of regional offices; the Agence nationale pour la valorisation de la recherche (ANVAR) -- which controls important resources for the stimulation and support of innovative activities -- has also considerably strengthened its regional bureaux. However, as in Finland, it is widely agreed in France that, at least at the initial stages, the development of an effective university/industry partnership depends very much on the "catalytic" function which key individuals can play.

But there are examples of universities stimulated by regions and especially by new technology-oriented enterprises, as in Germany with the case of Erlangen-Nürnberg in northern Bavaria, where a new Siemens electronics plant has given a new start to the natural and engineering sciences at the university; or in the case of the eastern region of the Land Northrhine-Westphalia, where the computer firm Nixdorf was quite important for the development of the new Gesamthochschule Paderborn.

3. University/Industry Relations in Less Industrialised Countries

The issues raised by consideration of university/industry relations in the context of the less industrialised OECD countries are very different. Universities established in less industrialised regions of countries such as Finland and France may be, as shown above, if anything more adaptive and innovative in their structures than those of the rest of the country. By contrast, the universities of the less industrialised countries tend to be rigid, hierarchic, traditional, and lacking autonomy with respect to their Ministries of Education. University research groups are often so small as scarcely to be viable. There is little or no external demand for academic research, since firms make little use of R&D and lack the capacity to absorb its results. Firms which are involved in mass production under licence tend to turn to their foreign licensors for help with any problems which emerge in the production process. Industry is not capable of adequately defining its problems in ways meaningful to scientists and may not even have problems amenable to scientific research. Concern is essentially with survival and short-term profit and there is little willingness to invest in R&D aimed at product improvement when the internal market can be retained without taking such risks. At the same time academics have not sought industrial contacts, but have preferred to try to build up scientific reputations through publication in the international scientific literature.

This is not to say that in such societies professors and industrial leaders do not know each other: it is often characteristic that in order to gain entry to the social elite the professor seeks to play other traditional roles. The contacts of professors with industrialists frequently occur only in this way and, consequently, there is little or no institutional impact. The result tends to be that informal relations exist, but remain irrelevant from the point of view of academic activities -- which does not necessarily mean that they could not provide a basis for new forms of collaboration.

The example of Ireland is usefully presented against such a background, for it is indicative of what can be achieved. In the last two decades a determined effort at modernisation and transformation has been made. A notable element of policy has been job creation through incentives offered to foreign firms to establish themselves (and more than 700 firms were established between 1960 and 1979). At the same time Ireland has sought to provide for indigenous industrial growth, and in this context many of the initiatives taken can be viewed in relation to university/industry co-operation.

Although new initiatives are discussed elsewhere in this report, it is useful at this point to refer to one which is significant particularly in relation to the level of development in Ireland. In the early 60s a National Institute of Higher Education (NIHE) was established with branches in particular in Dublin and Limerick. A central "interface" institution, the NIHE has attempted from the start to promote formal links with industry, in education as well as research matters.

These (and other) initiatives can all individually be described as successful, and yet co-operation between universities and industry in the view of Irish Authorities, is still far from adequate. Part of the problem is undoubtedly due to the slow industrial transformation: much Irish industry is not yet capable of absorbing the results of research. Where industry is strong and sophisticated and where a corresponding scientific capacity has been developed in the academic system (as in the Dairy Sciences department at University College Cork) then relations can be good. But given the increasing importance attached to R&D for future industrial change, obstacles which remain in the academic world become more and more prominent in discussions. There is for example the question of incentives to collaborate: recently introduced rules require that all remuneration for outside work carried out by a full time university teacher be deducted from his salary. This is seen as a major disincentive and a barrier to university/industry relations.

B. NETWORKS DEPEND ON THE SCALE AND BRANCH OF INDUSTRY

The relationships of large firms in research-intensive sectors with the universities (see the case of Switzerland discussed above) stand in sharp contrast to those of small and medium sized firms in traditional areas of industrial activity. The discussion will show that i) both the extent and the nature of university/industry relations depend upon sector and firm size; and ii) the objectives of such relationships -- the function which academic institutions can perform (more or less effectively) for industry -- similarly vary.

1. <u>Large Firms in High Technologies</u>

Some very large firms are intensely involved in research and development at the forefront of their respective technologies: their facilities for research, their investment in it, the calibre of the scientists they recruit are generally comparable -- and often superior -- to what is available in the universities. At least until recently such firms have recruited scientists and engineers on a considerable scale. It has been widely recognised in the universities that co-operation with them has much to offer: job opportunities for graduates, access to advanced instruments and facilities not available in the university, and (sometimes) support for research projects.

The contacts of such firms are far-flung: in France for example, Thomson-CSF has contractual relations with academic institutions throughout the country as well as abroad. It is one of the 100 firms participating in the Industrial Affiliates Scheme of MIT (a programme which enables subscribing firms to be kept regularly informed of the progress of research at MIT), and of which 40 are European. Giant research-based firms are more than willing to be involved in the work of the universities, to collaborate, to subsidise academic research. This is so for a number of reasons. It provides a basis for future recruitment: firms are anxious to ensure the quality and relevance of research training. Second, universities are tuned in to world-wide developments and may have easier access to emerging ideas (especially abroad); they have the time to pursue things in greater depth, and often at less cost, than is possible in industry. Research scientists employed by such large firms are encouraged to play an active role in the scientific community, international as well as national, through presenting papers, publication, etc. A company such as Thomson-CSF for example, recognises that although in some fields (such as materials, underwater communications) it may be more advanced than university laboratories, yet university scientists have the possibility of investigating questions of interest in much greater depth than is possible in their own laboratories. A real division of labour among colleagues often takes place, leading to many joint publications.

In so far as the development of the relationships of such firms with academia meet with difficulties, these seem largely to stem either from the relative underdevelopment of academic facilities or expertise, or from a lack of appreciation by university scientists of the real intellectual challenge posed by industrial questions. It is these two perceptions which largely explain the kind of initiatives taken by some large companies. On the one hand, these include the establishment of forums within which theme-based discussion between industrialists and academic scientists can take place on a free and continuing basis (the Clubs established by Electricité de France are an excellent example). On the other hand, there are a number of instances of large firms seeking to up-grade the level of academic research and teaching. The access to advanced equipment provided to Japanese universities by the manufacturers is one example. Another is provided by a programme of Northern

Telecom in Canada. Concerned by the poor and outdated equipment for educational purposes, the firm has established a programme wherein integrated circuits designed by students as part of their course work are fabricated by the firm and returned to the university along with test results.

It is important to recognise that the particular nature of these links depends not only on the size of the firms involved, but also on their R&D intensiveness, and the rate of technological change.

2. Large Firms in Traditional Sectors

Large R&D intensive firms and technical universities do entertain in certain Member countries (mainly the industrialised ones) long-standing, traditional connections. This is, for example, often the case in chemistry, electrical and mechanical engineering. But there are also many large firms active in fields in which technological change is less rapid, and in which market position depends upon factors other than level of technological sophistication. This is true, for example, in shipbuilding, mining and, with some notable exceptions, automobile engineering. Such firms are generally involved to a much smaller extent in R&D, and relationships with university research are correspondingly very much weaker. In the first place, part of the explanation lies in the traditions of recruitment, and the backgrounds of management.

Firms working in branches where technical change is slow are often major employers, and their difficulties in the current recession are a crucial political issue in almost all OECD countries. Their future is a matter of some uncertainty as some foresee the need for major restructuring. The political, social and economic magnitude of this problem dwarfs attention to university-industry relations, but it might be appropriate to take advantage of the current trend towards reorganisation to provide the new structures with some university-oriented organs. Firms can change: for example, it appears that Volvo is responding to the current economic situation by beginning to plan ahead in a more long-term, research-oriented, strategic fashion. The view in Chalmers University is that as a consequence, their links with the firm are becoming more fruitful.

3. Small and Medium Size Firms in High Technologies

The creation of a more effective inter-relationship between small and medium sized firms (SME) and the universities is a central focus of governmental interest in the subject of this report. But just as in the case of large firms, there are at least two situations and sets of issues. In the first place, much interest attaches to the fostering of small high technology firms in advanced sectors. Hopes, almost everywhere, are pinned on the production of high value-added goods (and services) by SMEs in new research-intensive sectors such as micro-electronics and biotechnology. Quite distinct, and raising different issues, are the needs of SMEs in long-established fields where technological process has usually been incremental.

In considering first the high technology firms there are, once more, two sets of issues raised by their connexions with the universities. First is the matter of the initial establishment of such firms, and the ways in which their "spin off" from university research can be facilitated. Collaboration or other forms of communication with the university in relation to the continuing viability of such firms is then, logically, the second issue. The fact is that in many OECD countries not only do education and culture of the universities frequently inhibit entrepreneurial activity, but the conditions of university employment virtually forbid it. In French universities (and France is far from unique in this respect), little is done to provide potential entrepreneurs (whether staff or students) with basic grounding in the economic financial and legal matters which pose major problems for the founder of a new firm. At the same time, it is not legally permissible for a university or CNRS employee to be, at the same time, a director of a private firm.

There are good reasons, relating to the proper use of public funds, why this should be so. Yet it may be that there are possible half-way measures (e.g. half-time appointment at half-salary, but with retention of title and status) which might be introduced. Elsewhere, steps have been taken precisely to assist university staff and students in setting up such firms.

Although there is much talk about the need to make university staff and graduates more entrepreneurial, to encourage them to seek to industrialise their ideas (whether through patenting and licensing or through company formation), policies have tended very much more to seek to meet the needs of such firms when once established. This is true for France where the lack of stimulation of entrepreneurial activity within the universities is matched by a rather favourable climate for the nurture of firms once existing.

Characterisation of the kinds of links with the universities which such firms enjoy, or need, can only be in the light of the activities in which they engage. This tends to be a mixture of production and services. Some of them are engaged in the fabrication of highly sophisticated components or products. The French firm Quantel, which makes lasers for research purposes, is a very successful example of a company founded by an ex-professor of physics. Others provide highly sophisticated services, for example -- and this may be a particularly crucial role -- as research sub-contractors specialising in scaling up or exploring for industry ideas developed in the universities from which they have come. Essential for all such firms appears to be close integration into the scientific community, national and international. Naturally this happens more easily where founders of firms are scientists of established reputation already. Successful firms thus tend to be those made up of young highly motivated and qualified professionals who have very regular contacts with the academic world.

Clearly from this point of view at least there are advantages in facilitating the foundation of firms by academics who at the same time retain their university position. Otherwise, firms sever their ties with the academic world may find it a real task to secure access to international networks of scientific communication. Some firms of this kind, especially those carrying out studies (e.g. those designed to bring an idea up to the prototype stage) in a rather broad field, find it difficult to keep up-to-date with the range of relevant university research. Needs in this respect may require rather more than access to data banks, for inevitably much of the necessary knowledge will be of the "tacit" kind which does not find its way -- and probably could not -- into printed reports. Moreover, firms providing research services or consultancy may have an additional problem of acceptance in that some in the universities will see them as competitors for contracts.

4. Small and Medium Size Firms in Traditional Sectors

It is in the need for effective interface institutions that the problem of university links with the bulk of SMEs is most specific. Effective connexions for the majority of them take place only through the effective operation of intermediaries. These, however, have not always been created for this specific purpose.

Building out intermediaries from the universities is a possibility which draws increasing attention. They may be institutions attached to -- or establish at -- the universities, in order to provide channels for easier contacts with industrialists. This is a function of Industrial Liaison Units or Officers attached to almost all universities in the United Kingdom, as well as the Transfer Points being established in the Netherlands. The idea of such liaison officers, partly to act as a switchboard directing industrialists seeking help to the most appropriate expertise, partly to go out and meet industry, has spread rapidly throughout OECD countries over the past decade. One of the most developed forms of the liaison office is to be found in the Ruhr area of Germany. "Unikontakt" (Kontaktstelle für Informationstransfer Universität-industrie, Ruhr Universität Bochum) provides a useful example for it shows first how the simple concept of a liaison officer may be developed, and at the same time the constraints which university structure may place on the effective working out of this role. Other German universities have followed this example. But experience suggests that the organisation is to some extent handicapped by the rigidities of the university structure; the administrative difficulties in handling research contracts within the universities; and the rather limited interest of university scientists in the short-term practical questions with which the industrialists are largely preoccupied.

Unikontakt (Germany)

"Unikontakt" functions in its most simple form as a switchboard, directing potential "clients" to the appropriate researcher or institute. But its function is also more complex. It includes: the attempt to initiate and find finance for joint university/industry projects; to procure advisory services and conferences and seminars to bring about a flow of information between the university and industry in the region; to aid in the obtaining and licensing of patents deriving from university research. "Unikontakt" is now a joint undertaking of Bochum and Dortmund Universities. An interesting aspect is its efforts to make university scientists more familiar with the rudiments of industrial and business practice.

It seems clear that "building out" from the university has to involve something more than the grafting of a liaison officer(s) onto a university structure. One aspect of this "something more" is readily identified. There seems no doubt whatever than an effective university initiative in the direction of SMEs must involve a combination of educational and research activity. Second, such initiatives must be directed principally at SMEs within the region of the university. There is naturally scope for a variety of educational aspects to the sorts of initiatives which the university seems usefully able to take. They may, for example, invite firms to suggest topics for masters degree dissertations (as at Chalmers University in Sweden); they may try to arrange industrial "stages" for students especially in local small and medium size firms (as is done in many places, for example in Canada, France, Germany, Ireland, the United Kingdom, etc.); they may develop and expand adult education courses (education permanent) in fields of industrial interest. Experience seems to suggest that it is through the educational route, through initiatives of these kinds, that industrialists come to acquire confidence in the university. Ideally the university tries to inculcate in its students, especially where these are already industrialists, a feeling that they acquire a future right to turn to former teachers for advice and for help. Adult education must thus include a deliberate attempt to foster permanent bonds between the university and the students who pass through.

In general, the planning of such activities takes place within a consultative body, regional in its scope, and on which academic and industrial organisations are both represented, perhaps also with representatives of community organisation and trade union groups. But the major point to be stressed here is the crucial significance of academic initiatives involving both research and teaching -- and the tendency of research collaboration to emerge out of contacts built up through educational work -- in developing good connexions with SMEs.

In many Member countries a quite distinct set of initiatives, which may be seen as the attempt to build outwards from industry, may also be identified. Such initiatives have generally sought to establish a source of advice on technical and professional matters which is easily accessible to small firms, which is seen to "speak the same language", and is not separated by barriers of status and esotericism in the way that universities often appear to be. There are many examples of such institutions, and though they have been established under many different auspices, experience seems to point generally to the important role which local or regional Chambers of Commerce play, or can play, in their establishment and acceptance. The work of the ARISTs in France is noteworthy.

The ARISTs (France)

This is a network of regional delegates established over the past five years, whose task it is to direct small firms to scientific and technical information required for problems identified in the course of their business. The problems with which SMEs come to ARISTs are not scientifically sophisticated ones, and generally the answers are to be found in the information banks to which the ARIST delegates have access. Questions tend to concern not only technical matters, but questions over markets, legal aspects of exporting, finance and so on. The ARISTs are closely related to, and often physically installed within, regional Chambers of Commerce and Industry. Thus, they are viewed by SMEs as created by their peers, for their own special use.

Similar initiatives have been taken elsewhere: in a number of Swiss cantons for example it has been the Chamber of Commerce which has been the moving spirit. In Finland the State Technical Research Centre (VTT) set up marketing units with similar responsibilities. Variants on this approach to building out from the world of SMEs are also to be found in Germany (e.g. the initiative of the Land Baden-Wurttemberg) and the Technological Information Centres in Denmark.

Standing between these two sets of institutions are a variety of organisational forms -- those generated from the university side and those which have emerged from industry -- which perform many crucial functions. For some of these, bridging the gap between universities and industry is not a principal function. Major government research establishments in high technology areas such as space, defence, telecommunications do nevertheless perform such a function though it is only implicit in their activities. On the one hand they are necessarily highly integrated into the research world, on the other they may be major customers for components, instrumentation and a wide variety of manufactured goods and services. Into the process of design and specification they will inevitably import the fruits of their collaboration with universities. Thus, it is noteworthy that in Toulouse (France) the implantation of a major space centre (CNES) has brought about some relocation of industry into the area and has stimulated a major improvement of university/industry relations around the city.

Another vital set of institutions in certain countries are those concerned with patenting and the licensing of inventions. In some cases these are public bodies, such as the British Technology Group -- BTG (previously NRDC) -- in the United Kingdom and the JRDC in Japan. The work of the Japan Research Development Corporation is illustrative, and consists of two types of activity: development by contract and licensing. In a number of other countries, bodies performing this function have not succeeded to the same extent in making themselves known in the universities and in encouraging university scientists to interest themselves in patenting and licensing the results of their work.

The Tasks of JRDC (Japan)

The first task of JRDC is to organise proposals for development projects and to select companies to carry out the work. JRDC bears the total cost of the project. If the development project is successful the company is authorised to commercialise the new technology under a new contract. The second task is to facilitate the licensing of patents held by public -- including university -- laboratories. Universities have a major place among the sources of the projects currently being promoted by JRDC through both of these procedures: more than half with respect to development, almost one-third as regards licensing projects.

A further set of institutions to be referred to here are the public sector contract research organisations, which themselves are of many types. Not only do they exist in a variety of legal forms, but their work is a very variable balance of basic research, strategic research, problem-solving and technical services (including testing). One example is the 20 or so institutes affiliated to the Danish Academy of Technical Sciences (ATV). These institutes (operating in specific fields such as acoustics, water quality, welding, toxicology) are self-governing under the Academy and exist largely to carry out research under commission for industry. They were introduced initially as a means of preventing the Technical University from becoming too involved in applied contractual research, but they are frequently situated in an industrial park near the University and they enjoy good contacts with it. A second and also highly successful model is SINTEF, an independent foundation attached to the Norwegian Institute of Technology in Trondheim.

SINTEF (Norway)

SINTEF earns the bulk of its income from contracts both to public and private clients, and in a wide variety of fields. The Foundation's work brings a degree of industrial relevance into the teaching and research of the Institute of Technology (NTH), and some of its own staff are involved in part-time teaching and research supervision. At the same time, Technical Institute staff may be involved in SINTEF projects and there is some joint use of laboratories and equipment. Moreover SINTEF provides career opportunities for NTH students and staff who may wish to move from purely academic to more industrially-relevant work. The connexions between SINTEF and the host Institute are in many ways a model of successful but informal integration.

Other institutional forms are not always so successful. Relationships with universities may be difficult, perhaps partly because the organisation and the universities may see themselves as to some extent in competition for contracts. It is not uncommon that even location on a common site fails to bring about effective and easy relations. Collective research institutions organised on a sector basis, such as the British Research Associations or the French Centres techniques, may sometimes fail to function as an effective bridge between the two worlds to which they are in theory connected. In France, for example, a survey showed that SMEs used the Centres techniques largely as a source of existing information and for routine testing, rather than for applied research. For their part, university scientists find the Centres unwilling to enter into any relationship with them, they tend to have a negative image of the Centres, and to be unsure whether a closer relationship would in fact serve any purpose. Remedies may often start with rather simple measures, such as appointing organisational scientists as visiting teachers or professors, allowing staff to use their work for higher degrees, and so on.

It is noteworthy that in France industry attaches considerable value to private research firms. These seem to perform a vital function especially for the more innovative among SMEs. So too it seems they are able to do for university research workers interested in working up their ideas to a stage at which they might be of interest to manufacturing industry. It is important to recognise that there is a major gap between the form in which university scientists tend to "leave" ideas -- for example in the scientific literature -- and the rather more developed form in which they can be assimilated by SMEs. These, unlike large research firms, are not generally able to do this working up themselves. French experience seems to suggest that this developmental process, which has to be conducted with some awareness of markets and industrial constraints and opportunities, may be most effectively conducted by private research firms which are a sub-set of the high technology SMEs, often established around universities, and requiring close integration into the world of public science.

II. HOW NETWORKS FUNCTION

The intentions of the various schemes discussed below are far from identical. Whilst all are of course addressed to the amelioration of university/industry relations, this general purpose allows for substantial variation in precise objectives. In functional terms, these schemes can usefully be grouped under the following headings provided it is remembered that, in most cases, these schemes do not have a single function, and that -- in fact -- the most ambitious ones tend to be multi-purpose activities:

-- Promotion of Long-Term Linkages Between Universities and Industry;

-- Promotion of Specific Areas of Scientific and Technological Activity;

-- Development of Liaison Systems.

A. PROMOTION OF LONG-TERM LINKAGES BETWEEN UNIVERSITIES AND INDUSTRY

The schemes which have to be considered here are in a sense the most fundamental of all, since they may often require a re-assessment of established procedures and values with respect to all university functions, including research and education. Put otherwise, the objective here is the development of an informal structure, and the means chosen may include reform of the structure of higher education. For example, attempts of the British government through the 1960s to establish a distinct sector of higher education especially oriented to the needs of industry (first with the Technological Universities, later with the Polytechnics) represented initiatives of this kind. So too do the policies of the Finnish government in establishing institutions of higher education in development regions (as at Oulu, Kuopio, Joensuu, etc.) with the objectives first of retaining skilled manpower in the region and second of stimulating a kind of refurbishment of the industrial structure. The discussion which follows is of necessity limited to a number of recent initiatives of this kind.

1. Incentives and Deregulation

Schemes of the kinds described above (which may be due to government, local authorities, industrial or university initiatives) far from exhaust the range of measures designed to bring about fundamentally new, and permanent, university/industry relations. Their significance perhaps lies at least partly in the fact that, addressed as they are almost exclusively to the needs of small firms in high technology sectors, they reflect a central focus of national concern in the majority of Member countries. At the other extreme, and based on an entirely different conception of an innovation/industrial strategy, are the indirect mechanisms preferred for example by the Federal Government in the United States. Equally intended to bring about an intensification of university/industry relations of a permanent kind, these measures are not selective in terms of the sectors to which they are addressed.

Recent United States Federal initiatives include larger tax credits for increases in R&D expenditure; further tax incentives to manufacturers of scientific instruments to donate these to universities; revised patent legislation so that small businesses as well as universities can profit through patenting of inventions deriving from Federal funds; revised anti-trust guidelines, so that collaboration of market competitors in a joint programme of research will no longer carry the danger of prosecution under anti-trust law. This in a sense protects and guarantees a number of initiatives already taken by industry and universities (which are referred to below).

There are, in Member countries, a great number of regulations and practices which hinder co-operation between university researchers and industry, for example those which limit the liberty of academic scientists to do paid work for commercial firms. Another factor, closely related, is the structure of the remuneration system for university personnel.

2. Science Parks

There have been a number of such initiatives over the past decade. Since the first was established around Cambridge in 1973, some 20 science parks are in existence, under construction or in the planning stages in the United Kingdom alone. The Heriot Watt Research Park which was set up in 1974 is the only science park in the United Kingdom on a university campus. Proximity to a university is desired largely because it facilitates day-to-day contact from which, it seems, enhanced creativity results. The concept of the science park is, of course, based on the assumption -- seemingly borne out -- that high technology firms prefer to (re)locate near to universities.

Many attempts to establish such centres of high technology activity have failed. The, by now, large number of failures as compared with successes has led to the belief that science parks are a result of a spontaneous evolution and that, because the conditions for success are so ill-understood, there is little that government (or anyone else for that matter) can do to promote science parks in specific locations. As opposed to this pessimistic view, and because it was the result of carefully developed policy and criteria (and so stands in sharp contrast to Route 128 or Silicon Valley) a good deal of interest attaches to the Research Triangle Park (RTP) in North Carolina (United States).

The Research Triangle Park (USA)

As early as the 1940s, Dr. W. Odum of the University of North Carolina believed that by pooling the resources of the three universities based in the cities surrounding the area now occupied

> by the Park, research activities could be initiated which held the prospect of transforming the economy of North Carolina which at that time was based upon the textile, furniture and tobacco industries. Initial development was slow, and after seven years the Research Triangle Institute and Monsanto were the only significant operations. In 1965, both IBM and the EPA Environmental Research Centre decided to locate there. Subsequently there has been substantial growth and there are now some 43 occupants, providing over 13 000 jobs. Occupants are, however, required to obey stringent planning guidelines. The smallest available site is 8 acres, and only 15 per cent of the land can be built on and then only with careful landscaping. Although a certain amount of light manufacturing is now permitted, RTP continues to operate essentially as a research park.

Knowledge of the factors governing these kinds of decisions on the part of high technology firms has become an important consideration in the development of State policies. Reviewing the development of the RTP, Silicon Valley, and Route 128, a recent Congressional Staff Paper comments:

"No single element is responsible for the seemingly spontaneous and spectacular growth of high technology industries in these regions. Instead, a combination of factors, including research and teaching activities at great universities, a rich endowment of labour skills, venture capitalists, high technology entrepreneurs, and Federal procurement activities in the area, are intermingled to provide the intricate fabric of a "creative environment" that underlie the economic dynamics of the region."

A variation on the idea of science parks is illustrated by the establishment by Control Data Corporation of a number of "innovation centres". Here the objective is to help entrepreneurs make successful transition to the realities of commercial life. CDC, usually in conjunction with local government, creates a large "shell" in which entrepreneurs rent space and can be supplied with a range of business services -- financial and accounting advice, secretarial, computer and copying facilities. The first such centre was established in Minneapolis-St.-Paul in the United States. The first one to be attempted in Europe is being set up in Enschede (Netherlands). Enschede is a city in a redevelopment region of Holland and BMF (as it is called) is being financed through the Dutch banking system, the Regional Development Authority and CDC itself. The unique twist in the Dutch case is that the new centre is being situated in close proximity to the University of Twente which has an excellent reputation for generating entrepreneurs and starting up new companies. The existence of BMF, it is hoped, will serve to forge strong and permanent links between the University and the commercial world.

3. <u>University-Originated Firms</u>

Just as many government initiatives aimed at the establishment of long-term university/industry relations focus particularly on the needs of small high technology firms, so too do a certain number of initiatives taken by the universities. An example is the establishment of a company by a university as an institution (i.e., rather than privately by a member of staff). Examples of such companies are not rare and vary in the extent to which they immerse themselves in a purely commercial environment. One example is Vuman, set up by the University of Manchester to act as a holding company. Vuman is a fully registered private company with a board of directors, part of whose function is to select likely inventions and to assist university scientists in developing their ideas to a point where they might be commercialised either by themselves or perhaps in conjunction with another firm.

The University of Saskatchewan's SED Systems Incorporated is another example of a university initiative aimed at promoting closer links with industry but it is more than that. It also illustrates that university-originated companies, like other companies, must diversify their product line and look to various sources for their finance.

SED Systems Inc. (Canada)

Originally set up to provide instrumentation for rockets, the company was incorporated in 1972 and its activities now range from the manufacture of components for use in space technology to a wide variety of sophisticated agricultural instruments. The company now stands on a broad financial base, the equity being distributed between the provincial government (42 per cent), university (38 per cent) and public (20 per cent). The university/government co-operation stems from a joint interest in creating high technology employment in the province. Spin-off effects are now being observed in the arrival of other small companies.

In Sweden, Chalmers Technical University (CTH) has taken a highly positive attitude to the creations of spin-off firms, fifty of which have been formed in the last decade. In a typical case, the university will facilitate such creations by providing space and access to equipment. More generally, CTH encourages its departments' involvement in product innovation. A special office has been set up to assist in the area of patenting and licensing.

Standing in sharp contrast to this kind of involvement by universities in the high technology business sector are those initiatives which have been addressed to the problems of non-research based firms. Examples which suggest that a widespread pessimism as to the possibility of a university contribution to the non-research sectors is not wholly justified are of some significance. Successful relations here, of which one example is presented below, seem to have two crucial characteristics. First, links are likely to be with local firms (and successful examples of this kind of collaboration seem to be a major achievement of at least some universities established in development regions). Second, links are likely to involve provision both of teaching and research related to the firm or sector in question. Indeed, research connexions to firms having no traditional capacity for or use of research generally seem to flow out of links deriving from training or retraining courses ("éducation permanente").

An interesting example here is to be found in the work of the University of Helsinki's Centre for Research and Training established in the city of Lahti. Part of the Centre's work represents a new and distinctive approach to professional retraining, in that the focus is no longer the individual professional, but the whole firm or sector. Indeed, the objective in such a programme may be nothing less than a major transformation of the working of an industrial sector. To this end research and training may be combined in an integrated programme involving numerous departments of the university (whose co-operation has to be obtained) as well as local (non-university) educational and training organisations. One project of the Lahti Centre is indicative of this approach (which has encountered some opposition on the view that the university was here attempting to step far beyond its legitimate social role).

Helsinki University's Lahti Centre and the Fur Industry (Finland)

One current project is concerned with the development of the fur industry. It derived from a perception by staff of the Centre that while Finland is a major producer of fur, much of the product is of low quality and, moreover, very little of the total output is made up into manufactured goods within the country. The project was initiated to help fur farmers improve the quality of their furs, and to extend its processing, thereby increasing added value and creating jobs. The project has four parts:

-- a training project, in conjunction with the vocational training centres. This is a three year course directed at training teachers, supervisors and designers for the fur sewing industry;

-- a research project, involving various scientific departments of the university, and Tampere TH aimed at improving the quality of fur through genetic, nutritional and other research. Some financial support from firms has been received;

-- economic research on world markets, in co-operation with Turku University of Economics;

-- a research and development project aimed at transferring technical know-how from the clothing industry into the fur industry. This involves collaboration both with Tampere TH and with the College of Art and Design and is concerned largely with improvement of manufacturing processes and machinery.

---

4. Long-term Industry-University Partnerships

The wide networks of contacts which large high technology firms enjoy with the academic community, throughout the OECD area, have been discussed above. Whilst firms of this kind generally have significant internal R&D, university research groups are often seen to be valuable both as an extension of this research capacity and as a kind of "antenna" -- more commonly referred to by industrialists as a "window on research". This is all the more the case when a common research interest exists, for it then becomes a central cog linked into an informal network through which scientific information is passed.

Historically, perhaps most particularly in the United States, support of academic research in general by industry has reflected an identification of the well-being of the academic community with the corporate interest. DuPont, for example, introduced its programme of aid to academic institutions in 1918, with the intention of helping to upgrade the general quality of university chemistry. At present, some $6 million are allocated annually in the form of free grants (of the order of $10 000 each) to selected university departments. Firms like DuPont and IBM also support substantial visiting scientists' schemes, where university scientists come to spend some time in the laboratories of the company. This concern of industry -- particularly in high technology sectors -- to seek to ensure the quality of academic work is still of significance. In the United States in particular it is this which explains the importance, and the success, of certain new developments.

It is thus in these industries that a new co-operative approach to the support of university research is emerging in industry. This has been facilitated by new guidelines on anti-trust law recently issued by the Justice Department, and is most marked in the computer industry. The two major factors making for this new approach (reflected in initiatives such as Stanford's VLSI program) are the impact of foreign competition and the manpower situation. Not only is there an acute shortage of graduates in computer sciences, but the equipment necessary for state of the art instruction has become prohibitively expensive. The Semiconductor Research Co-operation uses funds from firms making and using semiconductors to support university research of a long-term nature: the objective is both to ensure the performance of this research and to augment the supply of manpower. In the chemical industry also, the Council for Chemical Research has been established (despite initial scepticism). At the end of 1982, 128 universities and 37 firms (some from outside the industry) had joined. Funds are used to provide basic support for university departments of member institutions, the extent of support being related to PhD graduate production.

But it is also true that it is firms precisely in these areas which are most likely to take advantage of more specific inducements offered by government. The NSF programme of Industry-University Co-operative Research grants, initiated in 1978 is indicative. On a competitive basis, and taking account of peer reviews as well as likely industrial benefit, this programme funds projects proposed and conducted jointly by academic and industrial scientists on a cost-sharing basis with industry. The dominance of the chemicals, aerospace and computer sectors is noteworthy: then comes the electrical field (though not electronics), and telecommunications. It should be noted that IUC projects are of a long-term fundamental character: more so than typical industrial research. The nation's top 50 R&D companies account for 43 per cent of expenditure in the programme. More formal initiatives, such as the Co-operative Research Centers, also established by NSF, and to which companies may formally affiliate, seem also to work rather easily in these areas of technology. Polymer science and technology is a good example. NSF funding in this programme is provided on an annually diminishing basis: the MIT polymers Center was the first to become self-financing. It is worth stressing that experience with both these programmes has been that success largely derives from pre-existing networks of contacts such as occur more commonly in the science-based industries.

Similar motivations are, of course, to be found in other countries. In Canada, for example, there are a number of long-term industrial partnerships of which INRS Telecommunications provides an interesting (and successful) example.

INRS (Canada)

INRS is both a research institute and a post-graduate education centre in telecommunications systems jointly sponsored by INRS and Bell Northern Research (BNR); BNR is the research wing of Bell and Northern Telecom and is the leading privately owned Candian R&D laboratory in high technology. The Centre provides a bridge between the academic and industrial communities allowing industrial research and post-graduate education to exist and reinforce one another by a constant daily interaction under one roof.

It is important to note that, in this industrial partnership at any rate, each of the partners has its own distinctive objectives; they each want different things from the collaboration. For example, INRS's objectives are aimed at promoting the economic development of Quebec by influencing the creation of high technology firms in the telecommunications industry. It plans to achieve this by first creating a centre of excellence for post-graduate training and research in telecommuncations. BNR, on the other hand, want an "on premises" facility that will allow its staff to pursue programmes of research that will lead to advanced degrees. BNR sees that one way to accomplish this is to provide a centre of basic research capable of supporting and complementing research and development activities within BNR(5).

A rather differently motivated type of industrial initiative merits some attention here. Firms may seek to develop connexions with academic institutions in order to secure for themselves a share of the highest quality graduating students. This is perhaps most typically the case in fields which even today suffer from shortage of skilled manpower (notably the micro-electronics, telecommunications and computer sectors). It may also be typically the case with medium sized firms. The example of GTE, in the United States, is illustrative.

GTE (USA)

Though General Telephone and Electronics (GTE) is actually a very large company, it can be presented here because its concern with university relations is one more typical of smaller firms. Its major motivation is to secure an adequate share of the best graduates. Its various university-directed activities (which include corporate philanthropy and contract research as well as the initiatives described below) are directed at changing the image of the firm on campus. The company's FOCUS programme provides grants of about $25 0000 for high quality private institutions selected through a competitive procedure. This programme, which uses a panel of distinguished scientists to make the selection, enables GTE to be seen as acting for the interest of the academic community as well as to generate contacts with academic institutions. A second GTE scheme is the Industrial Undergraduate Research Participation Project. Here promising students compete to spend a ten week period in a company research facility, where their work is supervised by young faculty members brought in from high quality academic institutions precisely for this purpose.

B. PROMOTION OF SPECIAL AREAS OF SCIENCE AND TECHNOLOGY

During the past decade, as technology has once more become a significant element in government economic and industrial policy, university/industry relations have come to receive new attention. Such attention is to some degree circumscribed by the fields of technology -- and science -- in which such hopes are now almost universally vested.

What is new in many of these initiatives is not so much the attempt to formulate national programmes in fields such as information science, marine science, biotechnology, computer science (though these fields are topical and have attracted such government interest) -- as the mode of co-ordination sought. More than previously, these initiatives exhibit a renewed attempt to coordinate contributions from university, government and industrial sectors. In the cases discussed below, the new initiatives are clearly aimed at stimulating universities to undertake research which left to themselves they might not initiate.

1. Basic Technologies for New Industries (Japan)

The extent to which government involves itself in the detailed co-ordination and planning of national programmes varies considerably. For example, in Japan the general thrust of MITI's policy is to provide by means of an infrastructure and a general pressure for relevance, research which will allow Japanese industry to establish and maintain a firm technological base.

Basic Technologies for New Industries (Japan)

The task which is the responsibility of the Agency of Industrial Science and Technology (AIST) is performed, somewhat indirectly, by co-ordinating the R&D programmes of its own research institutes. AIST is particularly interested in developing within and between these institutes R&D projects rooted in close collaboration between university and industry. One element, then, in every institute's research programme is a set of specific projects aimed at one or another basic technology.

For example, the National Chemical Laboratory for Industry claims that under the "basic technologies" project it is researching into new materials, biotechnology and new functional elements, including fundamental research in membrane separation and materials; while the Industrial Products Research Institute lists among its research projects the evolution of research and development of advanced, highly efficient separation membranes. The interesting thing about this programme is that even though universities and industries are collaborating in it, there is no evidence that membrane technology has been designated as some sort of national priority as would be the case in many other OECD countries. Second, it should be noted that in Japan it is more usual, as is the case illustrated here, for universities to join an already established government/industry research programme.

2. The SERC Directorate Programmes (UK)

One of the grey areas of science and technology policy concerns the relationship between priorities and the developments of policies which effectively can co-ordinate action aimed at attaining them. The SERC Directorate Scheme is essentially a mechanism for designing and implementing research policies in areas of perceived national need. Each Directorate is aimed specifically at areas where existing mechanisms such as research grants, studentships, fellowships, etc., are regarded as insufficient to provide an adequate basis for the development of activity and where a more comprehensive and active approach to research and development is thought to be necessary.

The SERC Directorates (United Kingdom)

One characteristic of these special Directorates is that they have functions of their own as regards decision-making and implementation. This means that each Directorate has the authority to allocate resources by means of research grants, studentships and fellowships and, thereby, of implementing its own policy more or less independently. For example, the Polymer Engineering Directorate was established in 1976 to "mobilise the engineering-oriented skills of the universities and the polytechnics" and to help improve the performance of the polymer fabrication industry. This Directorate started by stimulating and co-ordinating R&D programmes in the universities and bringing them closer to industrial needs. The Directorate has established programmes of research projects at more than 20 universities, most of which are collaborative ventures between the university and one or more companies. The Directorate advises companies on how to exploit the existing research facilities and capabilities in the universities as well as carrying out studies of the state of various aspects of the polymer engineering industry.

However, each Directorate's existence is only transitory. From the outset, the research programme is developed from inputs from the customer and, as the programme develops, it is expected that the balance of funding will shift in the direction of the user thereby freeing resources for the establishment of another Directorate. It is, of course, a matter for the Council of the SERC to decide which areas it wishes to promote but at this level the scientific community is formally represented on all the relevant committees concerned with the co-ordination of national research policy. As a consequence, SERC has an evolving short list of priorities to which it intends to devote resources when they become available.

3. Special Programmes

The Dutch Programme in biotechnology stems from that part of the recommendations of the 1980 Innovation Memorandum which is concerned with "various ways of strengthening the infrastructure for innovation by means of increasing co-operation between institutes of higher education and industry, setting up mechanisms for technology transfer and providing assistance for small and medium-sized firms".

The new element in this initiative derives from one of the fundamental objectives of the Innovation Memorandum which aims to orient university research more towards industrial and social needs. As with the SERC Directorates Scheme, the Dutch Programme in Biotechnology has developed a specific mechanism which should encourage universities to develop their own priorities because access to the new funds made available under this programme are conditional upon some evidence of restructuring within the university requesting the resources.

The Dutch Programme in Biotechnology

Thus, resources for the biotechnology programme are expected to come in large part either from the research institutes or the universities that would carry out the research. New resources would be made available partly from the Ministry of Economic Affairs and the Committee for Science Policy of the Ministry of Education and Science. This extra money ranges from 10 to 40 per cent of the total funds involved in the programme. To gain access to this extra money for biotechnology the research institutes have to present their research programme to the National Biotechnology Committee which has to agree to the proposals and to what new money will be made available. Re-orientation of research priorities is, therefore, forced (albeit indirectly) upon the research institutes because the new activity has to be financed through the institute's own funds. Industry, on the other hand, is supposed to contribute or even pay for those projects of an applied nature which can be linked to a particular firm or group of firms. Gradually, it is expected that industry will contribute to the support of strategic R&D projects.

The "Alvey Programme", in the United Kingdom, also proposes a financial incentive, but it is primarily directed at industry, with the hope that university and government research teams will join in.

The "Alvey Programme" (United Kingdom)

The Department of Industry launched in 1983 a programme of research on four main technological areas -- software engineering, very large scale integration, man-machine interfaces, and intelligent knowledge-based systems. The key feature of the programme is collaboration between firms, government research establishments and academic institutions. Research carried out is funded by government up to 50 per cent in the case of industry, up to 100 per cent in the case of universities. It is expected the programme will cost about £350 million over five years, some £200 million being provided by government. A new Directorate has been established in the Department of Industry to co-ordinate the programme.

Proposals under this programme normally involve at least two industrial parties, but it is hoped that academic and government research establishments will also be included in consolidated applications. It is also planned to establish a communications network linking the main research centres involved in this programme.

In Sweden, a unique project was started in biotechnology in 1982 at the University of Uppsala. Here too new funds have been made available, but the key feature is that, from the outset, it was planned to achieve close integration of university and industrial research teams.

The Swedish Co-operative Programme in Biotechnology

The project is planned for five years starting in fiscal 1982-83. It is jointly funded by the Swedish Board for Technological Development (STU), the University of Uppsala and Fortia -- a major pharmaceutical company in Sweden. The total costs for the five years are estimated at SKr. 36 million. So far STU has set aside SKr. 4.5 million for the two first years. The most interesting aspect -- from a university-industry perspective -- is that the project will be carried out at a university department (for cellular research at the Wallenberg Laboratories) but the researchers engaged in the project will be employed by Fortia. The terms of employment are similar to those of university researchers in general.

4. <u>Co-operative Schemes</u>

The question of the initiation by universities of research in new fields of science and technology is of a different order from the government initiatives discussed above. The history of the development of the sciences, at least, is in most OECD countries bound up with their institutionalisation within the university system. Universities, uniquely, are able to provide for the manpower needs of an expanding science. Many have argued that the facility with which new fields of science are accommodated within the higher education system of a country, a measure in a sense of the flexibility, the innovativeness, of a given system is in an important sense also a measure of the quality of that system. This general issue is beyond the scope of this report. However there remains the most specific question of the extent to which universities should seek, in their development, to address themselves to the needs of new fields as embodied in industrial concerns. To this question, the remarks of the President of Rennsselaer Polytechnic Institute -- quoted earlier (6) -- are apposite. RPI has been extremely successful, amongst other things, in the development of work in the industrially-vital field of computer aided design and manufacture (CAD-CAM), and the lesson drawn here is that industrial benefit should properly be an outcome of developments deriving from the universities' fundamental mission in teaching and research. This indeed is the view to which most universities would hold and which their practice would generally reflect. To provide for the needs of a new field of science or technology has considerable implications for the university (in a way that, for example, meeting a need for advice on a technical problem does not) since it will frequently demand modification to the fundamental (disciplinary) structure of the institution. Universities therefore have to seek to balance the demands being articulated by industry with the possibilities of the (potential) new field meeting general criteria of the academic world. Industry makes many demands which do not correspond with the requirements for the establishment of a new field.

However, what is particularly significant about the present time in several fields is precisely the consonance between the views of industry on the one hand and academia on the other as to the fields which need to be developed. In the United States in particular, some of the most significant developments in furtherance of new sciences and technologies are in the truest sense a joint initiative reflecting a complementarity of interest. This is most notably the case in micro-electronics and in biotechnology. Many current United States initiatives are not readily categorised as either deriving from the university or industry, so that the listing below is to some extent arbitrary. As a university initiative, the current proposal of Cornell University to establish a Biotechnology Institute may be cited.

i) <u>Cornell Biotechnology Institute</u>

Cornell University is in process of establishing an Institute for basic research in Biotechnology as a joint venture of various parts of the University, several sponsoring industries, and the State of New York. Its initial focus is to be in molecular genetics, cellular biology, and cell production.

Participating companies are being asked to commit funding for six years, beginning with $125 000 in the first year and totalling some $2.4 million over the period. These funds are to be used to operate what is called the Core Program, as well as for the support of part of the Basic Research Program. Any patents are to be held by the University, with sponsoring companies granted royalty-free licenses.

Three elements to the programme are planned:

-- The Core Program will provide Institute members (firms) with access to new and accumulated knowledge in biotechnology through

>   conferences, the visiting scientist scheme, preparation of reports, etc.
>
> -- The Basic Research Program, which will be funded both from Institute funds and by seeking research grants, will involve faculty members, Institute staff and visiting scientists.
>
> -- The Visiting Scientist Program will provide opportunities for industrial scientists to participate as resident scientists in the programme of the Institute, working on the basic research programme. The idea is that when the Institute has reached its intended size, each firm will be able to send two scientists with support for his work (up to $30 000) provided by the Institute.

The Cornell proposal outlined above seeks to put together a consortium of sponsoring firms. The majority of recent agreements in the biotechnology area, many of which have received considerable publicity because of the vast sums of money involved, link a university with only a single firm. In the fields of micro-electronics and biotechnology the new (for the United States) co-operative approach to the funding of university research of industrial significance is, however, distinctly visible. The following examples are illustrative of new developments in an area where the knowledge base is very broad.

ii) Massachusetts General Hospital-Hoechst

In 1981 the German chemical company Hoechst announced a ten year $50 million grant to the Massachusetts General Hospital to establish a department of genetic engineering associated with the Harvard Medical School department. The work is not confidential, and the director of the new department has control over the research to be done. Research is published, subject to a 30 day review by the company. Hoechst can send up to four scientists per year to work with the research group. Massachusetts General Hospital/Harvard retain patents, with Hoechst being granted exclusive licenses for their use. Similar projects are planned for co-operation between big German industrial firms, German universities and institutes of the Max-Planck Society.

iii) Harvard University-DuPont

In 1981 the DuPont Company announced a $6 million grant to Harvard Medical School for research in molecular genetics. This work was to be done in the School's new genetics department, and the grant was conditional on a particular scientist (Dr. Philip Leder) being recruited to head the department. Here too it is claimed that the conditions of the grant in no way restrict the academic freedom of the researchers. Here also patents belong to Harvard, with DuPont granted exclusive licenses. DuPont stated that it did not seek to set the research goals for the group, but to contribute to basic research in molecular genetics upon which it could draw.

Patents resulting from the research will be owned by the University; however, DuPont may receive exclusive rights to their use through licensing arrangements.

Research supported by the grant will "provide access to new basic information and will supplement genetics research already underway at

DuPont". The company has been interested in the application of molecular genetics to the production of human interferon.

iv) Stanford Center for Integrated Systems

In the micro-electronics field industrial consortia, rather than individual companies, support a number of the major co-operative initiatives which have been launched in the last few years. There seems little doubt that the stimulus to this development has been in part a widespread concern at the effects of foreign competition in the field and in part an equally widespread concern with a shortage of manpower skilled in the newest techniques required by industry. This type of joint industrial effort at an early stage of the R&D process has often been described as "Pre-competition co-operation".

A well known example is Stanford University's Center for Integrated Systems (CIS). Here, a development committee, headed by the President of Hewlett-Packard, began recruiting industrial sponsors who would each promise $250 000 per year for three years, plus operating funds, to construct and run a design automation laboratory, fabrication facility, etc. Within a year 14 sponsors had been recruited. The objectives of CIS are i) to produce 30 PhDs and 100 MS graduates per year; ii) to do fundamental research relevant to the development of VLSI systems; iii) to provide short courses and workshops. Policy of the Centre is set by a university committee: a sponsors' advisory committee is consulted, but final decisions rest with the university.

A senior executive of Xerox, one of CIS' major sponsors, has explained his interest as follows:

> "Xerox's contribution to CIS is very small compared to what we are investing internally in the same kind of research. For little additional investment we enlarge our perspective by participating in a broad program of basic research. We envision opportunities for joint interaction with the university and with other companies, as well as the ability to recruit students. On a per-dollar basis it should be a good investment."

Industrial involvement in the initiatives described here, and indeed in the attempt to facilitate the development of new fields of science and technology in other ways not discussed here, is almost exclusively limited to large firms in the most advanced sectors. But though the initiatives described in the present section of this chapter -- whether deriving from government, the universities or industry -- are a very particular form of university/industry relations, their importance is clear. For it is these initiatives which, in particular, are addressed to the technologies which are so widely seen as vital to the future industrial well-being of much of the OECD area.

C. DEVELOPMENT OF LIAISON SYSTEMS

One development that has characterised university/industry relations over the last decade has been the establishment throughout the universities of the OECD Member countries of some kind of industrial liaison organisations. In some countries, even today, these organisations are hardly more than switchboards for enquiries, but in others (often stimulated by national or local government) fresh attempts have been made to build from the universities out towards industry, especially to small and medium-sized firms whose problems seem to have become a central concern for so many OECD countries.

In general, university-based industrial liaison organisations are university initiatives and there is little direct evidence of industry acting in a collective way to promote such organisations; though industrial firms, by requesting information or help of various kinds, provide evidence of a general "need" for some sort of liaison function. The reason for this is probably that each firm's information requirements are peculiar to it and therefore there is no incentive to provide this sort of development in a collective way. Another possible explanation is that when firms in specific areas feel the need for a more or less permanent channel of communication they will develop it themselves and thereby bypass the universities. There is some evidence, for example, in the research co-operatives opening up in the semi-conductor industry, that firms may be establishing their own liaison systems.

The liaison systems described below illustrate the importance of an entrepreneurial orientation in the successful operation of an industrial liaison organisation. In the cases of Holland and Britain, the liaison function is perceived as something which must be built up by establishing contact with industry rather than waiting for industry to "call-up". In each of the examples, particularly in the case of the Kanagawa Industrial Register in Japan, the emphasis is on liaison specifically with small and medium-sized firms.

1. Transfer Points

Perhaps the most recent attempt to develop in a comprehensive fashion a liaison function common to universities and government research establishments has taken place in Holland under the general recommendations of the 1979 Innovation White Paper. Transfer points are organised on a regional basis and function as link organisations between university research scientists and industry -- usually local industry. The vitality of these links is to a large extent a function of the vitality of the personalities in, and the organisation of, the transfer point. The idea of an organisational transfer point between universities and industry is hardly new and the Dutch universities seem to have been modestly successful in attracting resources from industry through it. For example, research contracts amounted to about 15 per cent of total university research capacity in 1980. Nonetheless, the current economic situation is putting pressure on the universities to look more widely for funds and some of these, in particular the technical universities, are being very enterprising indeed. For example, the Technical University at Twente has an enterprising transfer point and has demonstrated a continuous growth in external fundings since at least 1978.

Recently, a number of organisations have been established to promote technology transfer and entrepreneurship in the sector of small and medium-sized firms in the Netherlands. Although activities explicitly related to university/industry collaboration do not figure largely here, one exception relates to the recent decision to establish three micro-electronics applications centres. These are to be set up near, but not to be part of, universities. Their aim is two-fold: first, to provide services (including design and other soft and hardware support) for firms lacking expertise in handling micro-electronics; second, to organise and carry out product development in collaboration with one or more firms in areas of advanced technology. The idea here is systematically to exploit the expertise available in these areas by forming market oriented development teams of technical specialists and people from industry. It is hoped that these activities will lead to commercial results within five years.

2. Regional Brokers

A variation on the theme of transfer points -- a sort of mobile industrial liaison office -- has been established by the Science and Engineering Research Council in the United Kingdom. The Regional Brokers Scheme as it is called is directed explicitly at the problems experienced by small and medium sized firms in acquiring access to advanced technology. The brokers are given the task of contacting small and medium sized firms to inform them about SERC schemes and support. Although this scheme is still in an experimental stage and the area covered by the brokers is not yet nationwide, it is said to be making a considerable contribution to the dissemination of the SERC schemes themselves.

3. Industrial Register

In Japan a renewed and growing interest in the use of science and technology for regional development has led to new initiatives. For example, the Prefecture of Kanagawa has made serious attempts to organise science and technology support for small and medium sized industries in the region. In the Industrial Research Institute of Kanagawa Prefecture there are some 150 scientists and engineers working within a technical advisory programme carried out in co-operation with MITI to solve the problems of small and medium sized firms. Technical advisers can assist firms for up to 10 days free of charge and during that time the salaries are paid by the Prefecture. Additional work, however, must be paid for by the firms. Additionally, there are about 1 000 scientists and engineers registered in a "science and technology manpower bank". These can be used as consultants by the firms in the region. In this case, the firm is expected to pay all expenses.

4. Evolution of the Role of University Liaison Systems

As indicated, most universities now operate at least some kind of industrial liaison system but there have also been specific university initiatives aimed at making the wide range of knowledge present in the university available to industry. These initiatives are concerned variously with education, training, information and consultancy service, testing, contract research and so forth. It is probably not worthwhile listing the most recent initiatives in this type of activity because the form is well known, but it is perhaps worthwhile noting that in general the liaison function is being differentiated into a very large number of highly specialised activities brought about in part because of the growth in consultancy services generally. If the universities ever had this liaison function entirely to themselves, they no longer do so now and in the future it is likely that the pressure of competition will drive the universities into trying to identify as yet unoccupied market niches.

One recurrent problem in the liaison function which still appears from the university side concerns the degree of scientific work involved in a piece of industrial research. There are some who hold the view that the most efficient way to use university resources is to deploy them on projects with a high scientific content and that academics should not have their time diverted to problems requiring low calibre scientific inputs. If this problem is not solved, demands addressed to the universities by industry may be ignored or rejected for valid reasons giving, however, the impression that the university is not willing to co-operate. The more so when the reasons for the refusal are not explicit or when there is an appearance that the proposal has not been really considered. One positive step to improve the climate has, for example, been made by the University of Bergen in Norway which has established a procedure for the evaluation of the scientific interest of proposals: the evaluation is conducted by the institutes concerned.

5. Industrial Research Education Programme

There are very few instances (except in such special cases as business schools) of the university reaching out to industry with the skills it does best -- teaching and research training. Universities in most countries, while they continue to pay lip service to the problem of continuing education do, in fact, cater for students in the age group 18 to 25. In particular, there is not enough in the way of post-graduate courses aimed specifically at helping potential researchers to operate across the interface between university research and industrial development. In the United Kingdom, the SERC-sponsored post-graduate education schemes, particularly the Co-operative Awards for Science and Engineering and the Total Technology Scheme, go some way towards meeting this need but one would like to see more initiatives from the universities in this respect. A recent example is the industrial research education programme that is currently operating in Denmark. The diploma "Industrial Researcher" is approximately equivalent to a Ph.D. The programme which commenced in 1972 has so far produced about 100 graduates with numbers increasing in recent years in which about 20 students graduated each year. The aim of the programme is to supply Danish trade and industry with people who are, through concentrated post-graduate activities, qualified to carry out research and development activities, and utilise research results within industrial enterprises.

The Industrial Research Education Programme (Denmark)

The education is offered to graduates with a university degree provided their qualifications are deemed to be satisfactory. Graduates with some years practical experience in a research institution or industrial enterprise are preferred. The programme is administered by an industrial research committee set up by the Danish Academy of Technical Sciences. Financing is based upon agreement between the enterprises and the institutions involved, the State generally paying 50 per cent of the costs and industry the other 50 per cent. Normally the education comprises work for two years partly in industrial development departments, partly in research and development institutions; it is combined with supplementary studies and courses of planning, and implementation of industrial development on an advanced level. For a substantial part of the education period, the graduate carries out practical work in connection with real development projects, and this work is based upon the co-operation of at least one research institute together with one or more industrial enterprises. The programme aims at acquainting the graduate with the total process of development and at making him understand, and adopt a positive attitude to the problems of industrial development. During the remaining period of his education, the graduate takes part in courses relevant to the education project, visits relevant contacts in Denmark and abroad, and carries out compulsory private studies of general and specific literature.

D. FROM KNOWLEDGE TO PRODUCTS

University initiatives in this area are of necessity limited in scope. At their most ambitious they too, however, seek to combine dissemination of knowledge through training with work (research of a kind) designed to bring knowledge to bear on the more specific problems of firms. In so far as the successful transfer of knowledge to production will very frequently require precisely this integration of applied research and training (which in itself may require integration of training provided at many levels in a company or industry: managers, scientists and engineers, technicians, workers) the structure of higher education as a whole becomes a matter for consideration. The traditional university is beginning to pay greater attention to the specific technical problems posed by production processes or products under development. It is also true that universities, albeit slowly, are coming to pay more attention to provision of retraining courses for university-level scientists, engineers and managers. Yet, as indicated above, it is almost certainly the case that more is required. Provision has also to be made for retraining of technicians, skilled production workers, and the host of sub-university personnel vital to the introduction of a new product or process. In most OECD countries, education at this non-university level is provided in distinctive short-cycle institutions. It thus follows that far more co-ordination of effort between the two sets of institutions (as well as consultation with both sides of industry) is essential. Though there are examples of universities beginning to co-operate with short cycle institutions in their areas (for example between some universities and community colleges in New York State), universities are still too inclined to stand aloof. Systematic dialogue, co-ordination with more mundane and purely local institutions, appears to many in the university world as a blurring of its exclusive boundaries. Yet the fact is, as some of the examples given in this report show, that the concept of the university is flexible enough to accommodate such experimentation. Indeed, the concept of the Gesamthochschule, and similar notions elsewhere, are precisely the attempt so to expand the concept of the university. Enhanced dialogue with institutions providing for knowledge transfers at all levels seems vital to effective transfer of knowledge into production.

The ultimate test of industrial liaison must be the embodiment of research results in new products and processes which further the objectives of the firm. The range of mechanisms and institutions which have as their principal purpose the transformation of new knowledge into new products, services or processes is considerable. Some of them were discussed above and need only be referred to here. Spin-off firms, developing out of the university, are one example. Another, demonstrably vital to the successful transformation of university research into commercialisable knowledge in France, and perhaps inadequately considered elsewhere, is the private research firm. Patent legislation should also be considered here, although the complexity and variability in this matter precludes full analysis. One word on this issue seems necessary, however. There is considerable variation between countries (and in the United States between universities) in the scope for an individual university scientist to patent and to profit from royalties. Whilst the Swedish academic may hope to secure the total royalty paid by a licensing firm on his invention (whatever the source of the research funds which he used), a profit sharing agreement between the university and/or the body providing research funds (for example in the United Kingdom the British Technology Group acting on behalf of a Research Council) and the individual is the usual arrangement. In some cases the financial incentive is very small. But whatever the significance of any such incentive, the effect on the propensity of an individual to patent is clearly so culturally determined that no simple generalisation can be offered. Somewhat differently, agreements between universities as corporate bodies and firms providing funds for research are now a matter of considerable attention, notably in the United States, and especially in response to the large-scale contracts in the field of biotechnology (discussed earlier). An important aspect of this, and a matter on which major American universities take distinctly different views, is the question of exclusive licensing. Some industrialists claim that the economic utility of sponsoring university research depends very considerably upon the possibility of negotiating an exclusive licensing agreement. This view is not universally held in industry (and many of the major new agreements do not provide for this); at the same time some universities (e.g. Yale) have rejected the idea of exclusive licensing on principle.

Despite the importance of issues such as this, and the high technology sectors to which they have especial relevance, the subject of this section has another aspect of no less importance. The transfer of knowledge to production signifies, not only the knowledge produced in path-breaking fields of inquiry such as biotechnology, but also the vast amount of existing knowledge inadequately diffused through the industrial system. Quite distinctive steps have to be taken, and in some instances have been taken, to stimulate such diffusion. For example, there has been interest over a very long period in the United States in applying the extension model, so effective in disseminating the results of agricultural research into practice, to the sphere of manufacturing industry. A number of American states have taken steps in this direction. The tentative view is that the model is less applicable here. Yet it is not certain that, in modified form, the lessons of agricultural extension could not have relevance: no definitive answer can be offered as yet. Moreover, the localised information service provided in France through the ARISTs (discussed above) and directed in particular at small firms, is an extremely successful example of a mechanism for disseminating existing knowledge of diverse kinds through a local industrial structure. The dissemination of knowledge -- knowledge transfer -- is in essence an educational problem. The necessary education can be provided informally, on demand, as in the extension and ARIST models. Alternatively, it can be provided through the provision of short training/retraining courses, organised formally by universities, and tailored to the needs of local firms and their staffs. (And a recurrent theme of this report, that successful university links with industry at the research level often develop out of educational connexions, needs to be reiterated at this point.)

1. The Swiss Impulse Programme

One of the most comprehensive recent government initiatives addressed to the knowledge-transfer problem in its full complexity is the Impulse Programme of the Federal Government of Switzerland.

The programme was stimulated by a number of concerns, notably: shortage of skilled manpower in certain industries; the need for advanced retraining provision; diminishing profit margins associated with problems of developing and selling new products. The programme was directed towards industrial sectors felt to have inadequately absorbed new technology, and to which other industrialised countries were also paying special attention: data processing, electronics, and energy conservation.

The Impulse Programme (Switzerland)

The first stage began in 1978 with an overall budget of SF 50 million. It included: establishment of a Swiss Software School (with students recruited from among qualified managers); a Centre for Evaluating and Controlling Electronic components; aid for research and training for the watchmaking industry; foundation of a Swiss Institute for Technical Information (which would provide an information service to clients on request); and the organisation of training courses on thermal insulation of buildings as well as the testing of insulating materials.

In 1982 a second stage was launched, with a budget of SF 100 million over six years. This was to include establishment of a Management Data Processing School (to supplement the Software School); establishment of further courses in computer-assisted construction techniques; further courses in building techniques; and the development of sensor, adjustment, and measurement techniques.

As can be seen, the Impulse Programme is extensive. It is in fact aimed at filling gaps in the basic training provided in universities by emphasizing supplementary training from the trade associations, industrial groups and schools. Its implementation produces a feed-back effect for the latter, which are consequently reviewing their courses.

2. McGill University Value-Engineering Workshop

The Value-Engineering Workshop at McGill University is an in-depth analysis of an industrial product or process with a view to improving its design and/or performance so that it can be produced, or perform its task, at a lower cost. The idea of conducting a value-engineering workshop was introduced in the Department of Mechanical Engineering at McGill University in 1973, and it is the only one of its kind in North America open to final year students. The workshop operates in teams (comprising five students and a company representative) which work intensively over a number of weeks on a project submitted by the company representative, attempting to solve design problems and improve product process performance.

> The Value-Engineering Workshop at
> McGill University (Canada)
>
> To date, the workshop has helped about 70 companies to cut costs and improve their competitive position whilst helping students to learn to apply their textbook knowledge to practical problems in industry. For a reasonable fee (which covers the university cost in hiring an outside consultant to run courses and seminars) the companies involved have achieved savings representing millions of dollars. Examples include work for an aviation company on a costly fuel control system for aircraft turbine engines that had resisted change for 25 years. The results of the workshop are potential savings of C$135 000 in five years. Another project -- to improve the cost performance of a scavenger pump for a diesel engine oil system -- resulted in the team eliminating this pump completely and improving the design of the main oil pump instead. Potential savings to the company are said to be C$1.2 million per annum.

3. The German Pilot Programme for New Technology-oriented Firms

In Germany, the Federal Ministry for Research and Technology finances a pilot programme for the foundation of new technology-oriented firms (Modellversuch "Förderung technologieorientierte Unternehmensgründungen"). This programme started with DM 100 million and is planned for the period 1983-1986. In this incentive programme, the newly founded firms are also assisted by special technology-consulting institutions. The Federal Government hopes that this programme will also lead banks and venture capital companies to strengthen their contribution to this type of industrial undertaking.

The programme is implemented in six regions: in Berlin, Hamburg, in the Ruhr area, in the Saarland, in the south-west German region of the towns Karlsruh/Pforzheim and in Eastern Bavaria. In microelectronics, however, there is no regional restriction.

> Pilot Programme "Promotion of Founding New Technology-Oriented
> Firms" (Germany)
>
> The federal Government provides project-bound subsidies and also guarantees the risks of innovation projects in connection with the creation of technology-oriented firms. Subsidies are also given for smaller firms which want to strengthen their technological basis. In the first phase of preparation, subsidies amount to a maximum of DM 54 000 (which constitute 90 per cent of total financing. For special innovation projects, a maximum of DM 900 000 can be allocated (covering 75 per cent of the total financing).
>
> In the phase of production and market introduction guarantees for Bank credits are offered, up to DM 1.6 million per credit (80 per cent guarantee per credit).

The programme supports innovation projects submitted by individuals who want to found new commercial technology-oriented firms, and it is hoped that this will prove attractive for junior scientists in universities. Further subsidies are also available for existing firms with less than ten employees.

CONCLUSIONS

University/industry relations have entered a new phase in terms of goals as well as magnitude. The need to explore new forms of communication and collaboration arises partly from the pressure of competition on the side of industry, partly from financial stringency on the side of the university, and on the whole from the fundamental scientific and technological requirements of progress in many areas of research. University/industry collaboration is characterised by a complexity of traditional and new forms that reflect both the various types and states of industries and the various capacities, values and interests of higher education institutions. These aspects vary greatly between Member countries and, as a consequence, not only is it hard to draw lessons from the experience of one country but also the transfer of that experience to another context is extremely limited.

Thus, the following conclusions usually do not attempt to assign specific roles to governments (central as well as regional or local), universities and industry. They essentially aim to bring to light measures and decisions which should be taken, actions which should be implemented, even occasionally attitudes which should be changed. In other words, they attempt to identify "things to be done" but not necessarily to define precisely the "doer", who might vary in such a broad range of conditions as that which this report attempts to cover.

A. THE PREREQUISITES FOR SUCCESS

Academic excellence is an important prerequisite for successful interaction of universities with industry, and in particular with the large science-based firms. It is not, however, an absolutely necessary condition in spite of its importance. All types of higher education establishements can and do provide some services to some types of industry. However, the realities of international competitiveness contain a distinct technological dimension which obliges industry to turn increasingly to the most up-to-date knowledge and highly qualified manpower available. Moreover, in a substantial number of areas, scientific interests and technological needs correspond closely.

On the industry side, clear articulation of needs is essential for a constructive relation with the world of science and technology. In many cases (notably on the part of the most sophisticated industries) this does not raise problems. In many instances, however -- small and medium-size firms, large traditional industries -- the formulation of an articulate industrial demand is, in itself, a concern. The involvement of university scientists, at an early stage in the identification of problems, often therefore proves useful.

This means that, from the points of view of industrial needs, fundamental research can coexist in higher education systems with research of a more strategic (but still long-term) nature, with targeted research, with shorter-term projects, and even with scientific and technological services.

It remains that each type of "university" must take stock of the proper balance to be maintained between its different activities so as not to compromise its basic functions. In each case, specific measures and adjustments will have to be made. However, in general, it is felt necessary to encourage university scientists to become more receptive to industrial demands. Thus:

-- the evaluation of projects and individuals which determines funding and careers could take more positive account of aspects of research design, implementation and follow-up which respond to industrial concerns, rather than stick to strictly scientific considerations;

-- government authorities could develop a more systematic overview of scientific and technological activities in universities (from research to services) in order to safeguard the balance and flexibility of the system;

-- efforts made by governments can also play a catalytic role in bringing together scientists and industrialists for the discussion and identification of problems which have a technological dimension.

The concomitant of this is that the most successful schemes are those which manifest the greatest degree of flexibility. Just as the ultimate application of a new technology is often not in the market originally seen by its first proponents, so too the most effective forms of university/industry relations are not always embodied in the original conception of them. Without flexibility, the evolution of collaboration via mutual interaction of stimulus and response atrophies. It is for this reason that it is often difficult to identify the source of a particular initiative or to assess its "success" by relating the outcome to the original expectations.

The possibility of shifting the central focus of a particular form of industry/university collaboration from education to retraining of highly skilled personnel and subsequently to research must be kept in mind.

-- Adequate administrative and budgetary measures will ensure the required flexibility in this respect and enable the universities to enter with industry into as broad and diverse a range of co-operative agreements as possible.

-- Member countries should identify regulations which diminish flexibility, at the institutional and individual levels, in responding to industrial requirements.

-- One of the most apparent sources of rigidities in some Member countries is, in particular, the difficulty for academics and industrialists to move, even for brief periods of time, from one sector to the other. Various schemes can facilitate and encourage short-term or medium-term mobility.

Flexibility in university/industry relations is most often the result of the efforts of single individuals operating with the minimum of organisational restrictions. As the innovation process itself is seen to depend critically on entrepreneurs or product champions, so too successful examples of university/industry relations always bear the stamp of some catalytic individuals who are able to hold their respective partners and institutions in dialogue until they are sufficiently comfortable with one another to get on with the problem in hand.

The fact that many examples of industry/university interaction rely on the initiative of individuals makes it a process which is difficult to predict and plan. However:

-- It has been very useful for governments to appoint or second dynamic individuals at key points (regional government organisations, professional societies, university or industrial consortia, etc.) where they can be encouraged to promote initiatives.

-- Central authorities could make a particular effort to detect infant initiatives and encourage them. Many failures may be required before a successful undertaking takes off and before a talented "entrepreneur" succeeds in mobilising others around him.

It is, of course, difficult to generalise from this type of experience. Each Member country has a particular set of institutions of higher education and a particular industrial complex; the patterns of university/industry relations reflect this particularity. It follows from this that there is no single model to describe effective university/industry collaboration: much depends on the needs of firms whose interests are to be served as well as on the capacities of the university system to provide for them. It is also clear that, given the diversity of needs which an extensive and differentiated industrial system manifests, the capacity of the university to initiate and to respond adequately will be intimately related both to its own traditions and to the role it sees for itself, or the niche it is trying to carve out, in that system.

In each country, a detailed analysis of the industrial structures, attitudes and opportunities is needed to clarify conditions to be met by industry in order to facilitate the establishment of a continuing and constructive relation with universities, in line with the national industrial strategy followed by the country in question.

It remains that, in all cases, the collaborative arrangements which have seemed to be most appreciated by all parties have been based on:

-- The existence, within the firm, of a long-term planning effort and an articulated strategy for growth.

-- A management structure in the firm which would not exclude external advice.

-- A willingness actively to pursue the recruitment of the highest possible level of qualified personnel.

-- An understanding of the "university ethos" regarding exchange of information, diffusion of results, etc.

Many universities do not wait passively for industry to present them with enquiries, demands and opportunities. They seek a new role, and they also take the initiative, often with the support of public authorities.

-- Various efforts, ranging from "science shops" to "open days" and seminars for the local business community can be launched and pursued systematically to initiate a dialogue.

-- Industrial liaison services can be established within universities to serve as a sensing and questing service oriented towards the industrial world. Such services may require, in order to be effective, administrative and budgetary resources which should be available on a permanent basis.

From the point of view of governments, the primary objective of university/industry relations is generally to contribute to the national economic performance by enhancing -- and perhaps accelerating -- the process of technological innovation. For industry, it usually means access to adequately trained personnel, to scientific and technological information, occasionally to research results. For the universities, it is -- of course -- a potential source of resources (funds as well as equipment), and there seems to be an increasing sense that one of the functions of universities is to contribute to regional -- and thereby national -- development. Finally, for the research scientists, stronger relation with firms which have been pioneers in certain disciplines is often seen to be a necessity from the point of view of research.

These relations may prosper provided initiatives are encouraged (and do not have, as noted above, to survive in a hostile administrative environment) and take account of the specific goals and constraints of each of the parties involved so that their basic functions are not compromised, while recognising that there is something to gain for each.

-- Incentives can be put in effect, for the benefit of firms involved (fiscal incentives, measures aiming at promoting retraining of industrial scientists, engineers and technicians, etc.).

-- Other incentives can prompt the university to seek industrial contacts and contracts (for example the possibility to apply for patents and grant licenses, to negotiate compensation for "overhead costs" in research contracts, etc).

-- Government funding will, in some cases, provide attractive "matching" opportunities for industry to invest in joint research and/or education programmes with universities; when the industry involved consists of small firms or large traditional ones, these undertakings are rarely to be expected to "pay their own way".

-- The conclusion of research contracts between universities and industry should, as much as possible, be left to the parties involved. However, they should be encouraged to pay due attention to the ethical aspects involved and, in particular where universities are concerned, to strengthen control mechanisms.

-- Certain forms of incentives and rewards are more specifically of concern for individual scientists. Private interest can coincide with the interests of society, and academic research workers often obtain, through patents and/or fees and other advantages, some compensation for their contributions which is considered quite legitimate in many countries.

B. UNIVERSITIES AND INNOVATION

The problems faced by a firm in relation to innovation depend, critically, upon its position in the innovation cycle; that is, whether it is at the beginning or the end of its technological learning curve and whether it is a large or small firm or in a transition between the two. On the basis of the evidence presented in this report -- "what roles have the universities played in relation to innovation and what are the prospects for the future?" -- four elements of the innovation cycle can be considered, where the universities have a distinct role to play.

1. Starting new companies

New companies are the life blood of any industrial system. Through them new ideas are brought nearer to the point where their ultimate commercial success can be gauged. It is clearly not a prime function of the university to seed the economy with new firms. Yet the translation of scientific ideas into industrial products functions is a powerful image for those who wish to justify public support for university research. Whether the justification is rhetoric or not, some universities have set up organisations to help both academics and non academics carry research results closer to the market place. In this respect, the universities function as "incubators" of innovation by assisting innovators to acquire the requisite management and financial skills.

Surprisingly enough, assistance to infant industrial firms seems to be exceptional in the array of mechanisms and procedures developed to assist in the development of high technology industries in Member countries.

-- "Incubator factory" schemes designed by some universities to assist new firms through the provision of space, management, financial and marketing skills have been tried with some success.

-- University leaders and government officials who seek to promote industry/university relations often overlook the potential contributions of business and commercial schools.

-- Technical assistance to product development may be required and may, in part, be provided by universities or organisations attached to it. Such spin-offs from universities ocasionally include technical assistance companies set up on a commercial basis and which have often turned out to be both quite effective and viable.

-- The issue of actual university involvement in the financing and management of new firms remains a debated one in many countries. In some cases, however, universities and university staff have been involved in the provision of venture capital required by colleagues who founded new firms.

2. Assistance to small, growing companies

Here, companies are generally in need of a wide range of expertise from technological advice through to marketing knowhow. The problem for firms in this phase of the innovation cycle is that their needs are so specific that it is not always possible for universities to organise their activities to deal effectively with them. At this stage what is required (and, to a large extent, it is what exists) are different forms of liaison systems which can quickly and effectively route enquiries through the university or to other institutions, and bring problems to the potential problem-solver. Many universities have such liaison systems; their success is critically dependent on both support from the highest level within the university and on the quality and enthusiasm of those who run them.

Many efforts to promote growth of high technology industries have focused on small and medium size firms. Universities are expected, at both regional and national levels, to contribute to the implementation of this policy. This may involve, in particular, the participation of university scientists (but not necessarily within a university setting proper; specialised institutions outside the university can draw upon university resources) in providing:

-- quality control, evaluation and testing services;

-- scientific and information services, both of a general nature and regarding highly specific technological areas.

However, the mismatch between the general capabilities of universities and the highly specific needs of small firms have limited and will continue to limit the possibilities for direct collaboration. Yet, universities have occasionally succeeded in initiating co-operation with small firms through various mechanisms:

-- the placement of graduate students in an industrial environment, under "sandwich course" types of programmes, has been very useful in this respect and has been the source of many permanent contacts;

-- students have also been usefully encouraged to undertake, as part of their training, the solution of industrial projects under the supervision of both their professor and the manager of the firm concerned;

-- opportunities for contacts are mainly realised when academic personnel benefit from statutes which make them available as consultants and allow them to be remunerated for these services;

-- various forms of industry/university co-operation have been stimulated by the creation, often on a regional basis, of "industrial consortia" which are in a better position than their individual members to express research demands to the university and interact with it;

-- finally, industry/university co-operation is not always direct and may flow through various intermediary and collective research bodies who should be encouraged to look to university contributions.

3. Collaboration with large, science-based firms

In this type of collaboration, both universities and industry are usually operating at the forefront of research and play a part in an international network of activity. Relations between these types of firms and the universities, then, must depend on the excellence of the latter and on developing an ethos of "equal partners" in research. Links between these firms and university are often to be made with individual scientists of high standing and, in some cases, industry has invested large sums of money in specific university departments to "formalise" relations between the parties. These forms of collaboration are often in areas of new technology and, therefore, both the universities and industry can benefit additionally from large government programmes specifically aimed at promoting new areas of research. However, it is worth noting that if a series of technical problems is perceived by industry as sufficiently basic to constitute a major generic research question, companies can, and often do, combine to develop specific research links with universities.

One of the salient features of the connections between this type of industry and universities is their long-term aspect, potential for continuity, and variety:

-- continuity can be maintained if the relationship starts on a sound basis from the point of view of the various parties (including university administration, individual scientists, industry officers and scientists, etc.). To avoid arrangements which could disrupt other university functions or prove inimical to university concerns, it may be advisable to spell out a code of proper conduct in this area;

-- governments can be involved in many ways, and it may be useful, in consultation with industry, to determine areas where public funds can play a "seeding function" through the provision of advanced facilities and equipment;

-- an increasing number of industry/university co-operative arrangements involve public research establishments; in many instances, the latter need to be encouraged to participate in such efforts;

-- the development of international industry/university co-operation is one of the important new trends in this area which raises many issues which have not yet been fully explored.

4. Assistance to mature industries

Mature industries may be large or small but this stage of the innovation cycle may be the most difficult within which to foster university/industry relations. Frequently, unable to interest government or to attract high quality graduates, these firms seem to be set on a path of inevitable decline. Such firms may need more, not less, investment in R&D and require more, not fewer, highly qualified graduates in their workforce. It is in this area where new approaches are often required with respect to the recruitment of qualified personnel, and where much greater effort is needed, to identify how academic capabilities can be directed to revitalising these industries and help in the often socially and economically painful process of introducing available new technologies in these industries.

One key problem in this area is related to the difficulty of initiating linkages between "old" industries and traditional universities which are often located in the same regions. In many instances, the interest will be in applying new technologies to improve the production and competitiveness of industry. On the university side, contributions may therefore often originate from engineering rather than science departments.

- -- The restructuring of certain industries currently under way in some countries should include plans for bringing industrial research and universities closer, from a geographical as well as institutional perspective. Regional and local authorities can play an essential role in this context.

- -- In many cases, the inclusion of engineering education and technological research on campus has done much to modify the general outlook of a traditional establishment of higher education.

- -- Here again, "sandwich courses" and retraining for highly qualified scientific and technological personnel open the way to new relationships.

- -- In almost all universities, even the most traditional, there exist some example of collaboration with industry, which may provide an example for others to follow or to join, provided its advantages, disadvantages and characteristics are openly discussed.

- -- The development of industrial liaison programmes has often started, from the university side, with efforts to organize increasing informal contacts (through social occasions, seminars, etc.) with industry.

- -- On the industrial side, management should seriously consider the setting up of university liaison services whose tasks would be to initiate contacts with university groups. It would be understood that this will be a long-term, progressive process which should not, from the outset, aim at excessively ambitious goals such as research contracts, but essentially strive to open channels of communication and create a climate of mutual confidence.

C. STRENGTHENING THE SOCIO-TECHNICAL COMMUNITY

In the universities of the Member countries collectively, then, schemes aimed at promoting collaborative work with industry at every phase of the innovative cycle exist. But Member countries are a long way yet from the complete establishment of a comprehensive socio-technical community in which individuals belonging to all types of private and public institutions operate in relative familiarity with each others' problems and needs. There is still a need to break down barriers to the flow of information between different institutions and sectors if the available expertise is to be mobilised to meet the social and economic challenges of the day. What is at stake, in fact, is the creation in a given region or even a nation, of a sense of community and shared interests (both intellectual and professional) among university personnel, industrial scientists and engineers, business and regional leaders, etc. -- in other words, the development of a socio-technical community -- so that individuals belonging to different sectors and "speaking different languages" learn to interact fairly routinely.

For the university personnel, however, this often calls for new attitudes towards the economic and social worlds off campus. The potential for developing these new attitudes among the university staff, those engaged in research as well as those engaged more extensively in education and special education programmes, is largely determined by career prospects and by the ways in which the professions in question are organised.

Thus, the constitution of socio-technical communities must take account of many factors, mostly attitudinal, some of a more logistical nature, relating to the academic world and its ethos in the strict sense, as well as to its involvement in non-academic life.

-- University career structures and, therefore, evaluation systems can ensure that researchers' involvement in non-academic affairs entails rewards rather than penalties in their subsequent professional development.

-- University research scientists should be encouraged, through funding mechanisms as well as efforts to involve and interest them in planning efforts, to design projects whose implementation and results might be relevant to local, regional and national concerns.

-- Conversely, it is important that industrialists be involved in academic planning and decision-making; they will thus become more directly acquainted with what is being done and can influence future orientations.

-- Interaction between representatives of all parts of the research system (various firms and higher education institutions, collective research bodies, etc.) is vital. "Science Parks" provide a favorable environment in certain conditions (geographical proximity, possibility to share facilities and skills, etc.) and can be conceived at various scales and stages of the R&D, innovation and production processes.

-- The identification of areas of overlap between scientific and industrial interests can provide an opportunity for informally bringing together scientists of different institutional backgrounds, through the establishment of "clubs".

-- On a continuing basis, it would be ideal for each scientific institution to be part of regional and national networks of person-to-person contacts. Reforms of higher education could strive to strenghten the "Master/Student relations" and mechanisms and incentives devised to encourage Alumni Programmes.

-- Regional policy-makers, professional societies, industrial organisations, etc., also have a key role to play (and could be offered government support in terms of both funds and skilled personnel for this purpose) to contribute to the creation of such networks.

Obviously, in the light of all these rising expectations, changes in the reward system for universities are necessary, and if universities do not prove capable of making a more systematic contribution to national industrial life, other non-university institutions will grow up to do the job for them. Indeed, in some Member countries, public institutions already perform such research activities outside the university context. These institutions, if their numbers continue to grow, will surely limit the possibilities for universities to become more directly involved in the industrial life of the country.

In the light of the economic and social challenges of our times, most -- if not all -- institutions must adapt and change rapidly. However, the management of change is much more difficult in institutions -- such as universities -- that possess a tradition which deeply affects the collective and individual behaviour of their members. Throughout the 1960s new social goals for the higher education sector were achieved, in part, by creating new institutions. By the end of the 1980s, the distinction between new and traditional institutionswill become increasingly blurred, and the pace of change will be a function of the ability of established institutions to adapt to new situations. A sobering thought on which to end this report.

NOTES AND REFERENCES

This report is about new forms of collaboration and communication between industry, universities and other institutions of higher education. The added precision is important because not all such institutions have as their aim the promotion of fundamental research in sciences; many, for example the polytechnics in the United Kingdom, were established with the expressed purpose of developing a capability in one or other area of applied science or technology.

The Future of University Research, OECD, Paris, 1981.

Canada, Denmark, Finland, France, Germany, Ireland, Italy, Japan, Netherlands, Norway, Sweden, Switzerland, United Kingdom and the United States. Copies can be made available, within the limits of supply, on request.

The Research System, Volume II, OECD, Paris, 1973, pp. 144-147.

The INRS/BNR relationship is governed by a contract which is renewed every five years. The contract governs the handling of publication rights, patents, access to technical information and facilities. It stipulates that the Institute may retain a certain number of BNR staff according to a formula based on the number of INRS personnel. The Institute has presently 33 industry and 42 university personnel.

See Introduction.

INDEX

	pages
-- Academy of Technical Sciences (ATV) Denmark	32
-- Agence nationale pour la valorisation de la recherche (ANVAR) France	24
-- Agences régionales pour l'information scientifique et technique (ARIST) France	30-52
-- Agency of Industrial Science and Technology (AIST) Japan	41
-- Alvey Programme United Kingdom	43/44
-- Basic Technologies for New Industries Japan	41
-- Biotechnology Programme Netherlands	43
-- British Technology Group (BTG)	31-52
-- Catalysts	22-24-57-58
-- Centre for Cold Ocean Resources and Engineering (C-Core) Canada	15
-- Center for Integrated Systems (CIS) United States	47
-- Centres techniques France	32
-- Chalmers Technological University Sweden	18/19-27-30-37
-- Clubs	26-64
-- Collective Research	31/32-60/61
-- Continuing Education	30-37-40-52-59
-- Co-operative Awards in Science and Engineering United Kingdom	50
-- Co-operative Programme in Biotechnology Sweden	44
-- Co-operative Research Centers United States	39
-- Cornell Biotechnology Institute United States	45/46
-- Council for Chemical Research United States	39

-- Diffusion of Research Results	20-25-26-30-47/51-51/55-57-60-62/63
DuPont de Nemours	39-46/47
-- Electricité de France	26
-- Evaluation	39-49/50-56
-- Federal Institutes of Technology Switzerland	20
-- General Telephone and Electronics (GTE)	40
-- Government Research Institutes	31-41-65
-- Harvard University-DuPont Project United States	46/47
-- IBM	39
-- Impulse Programme Switzerland	53
-- Incentives	41/44-51/52-59-62/63-64
-- Industrial Consortia	36/37-39-47-61
-- Industrial Funding of Research	12/13
-- Industrial Register Japan	49
-- Industrial Research Education Programme Denmark	50/51
-- Industrialising Countries	24/25
-- Informal Networks	13-20/21-25-38/39-62/65
-- Institut national de la recherche scientifique (INRS) Canada	40
-- Instruments	13-26/27-59-62/63
-- Japan Research and Development Corp. (JRDC)	31
-- Lahti Center of Research and Training Finland	38
-- Liaison Officers	20-21-29/31-47/51-51/55-57-60-62/63
-- Massachusetts General Hospital-Hoechst United States	46
-- McGill University Canada	53
-- MIT United States	18-26-39
-- Technical University of Munich Germany	18
-- National Institute of Higher Education (NIHE) Ireland	25
-- New Universities	19-22/23-34
-- Northern Telecommunications Canada	26/27
-- Patents and Licenses	28-31-35-46-59/60
-- Pilot Programme for New Technology-oriented Firms Germany	54/55
-- Quantel France	28

- -- Regional Brokers
    United Kingdom — 49
- -- Regional Development — 18-21/24-35-40-49-56-59/60
- -- Regulations — 27/28-35-57
- -- Rennsselaer Polytechnic Institute
    United States — 14-45
- -- Research Associations
    United Kingdom — 32
- -- Research Companies — 28-32/33-37-51/52
- - Research Triangle Park (RTP)
    United States — 35/36
- -- Sandwich Courses — 29-62/63
- -- Science and Engineering Research Council (SERC)
    United Kingdom — 21-42/43-48-49
- -- Science Parks — 18-35/36-64
- -- SED Systems Inc.
    Canada — 37
- -- Semi-conductor Research Co-operative
    United States — 37
- -- SERC Directorate Programmes
    United Kingdom — 42/43
- -- Siemens — 18-19-24
- -- SINTEF
    Norway — 19-32
- -- Small and Medium Size Firms — 18-20-21-25/26-27/33 49-56-57-61/62
- -- Spin-off Companies — 36/37-51/52-60
- -- Stanford University
    United States — 18-38/39
- -- Tax Policy — 36/37-59/60
- -- Technical University of Twente
    Netherlands — 36-48
- -- Technical Research Centre (VTT)
    Finland — 31
- -- Technology Information Centres
    Denmark — 31
- -- Thomson-CSF
    France — 26
- -- Total Technology Scheme
    United Kingdom — 51
- -- Training — 18-26/27-37/38-40/41-47-51-52-53-59/60-61
- -- Transfer Points
    Netherlands — 48
- -- Unikontakt
    Germany — 29
- -- Université de Grenoble
    France — 18
- -- Université de Haute-Alsace
    France — 18
- -- Université du Languedoc
    France — 15

-- Université Louis Pasteur
   France   18
-- Université technologique de Compiègne
   France   18/19
-- University of Bergen
   Norway   50
-- University College Cork
   Ireland   25
-- University of Joenssu
   Finland   22-34
-- University of Kuopio
   Finland   19-22-34
-- University of Manchester
   United Kingdom   36
-- University of Oulu
   Finland   19-22-34
-- Value-Engineering Workshop
   Canada   53
-- Volvo
   Sweden   27

OECD SALES AGENTS
DÉPOSITAIRES DES PUBLICATIONS DE L'OCDE

ARGENTINA – ARGENTINE
Carlos Hirsch S.R.L., Florida 165, 4° Piso (Galería Guemes)
1333 BUENOS AIRES, Tel. 33.1787.2391 y 30.7122

AUSTRALIA – AUSTRALIE
Australia and New Zealand Book Company Pty. Ltd.,
10 Aquatic Drive, Frenchs Forest, N.S.W. 2086
P.O. Box 459, BROOKVALE, N.S.W. 2100. Tel. (02) 452.44.11

AUSTRIA – AUTRICHE
OECD Publications and Information Center
4 Simrockstrasse 5300 Bonn (Germany). Tel. (0228) 21.60.45
Local Agent/Agent local :
Gerold and Co., Graben 31, WIEN 1. Tel. 52.22.35

BELGIUM – BELGIQUE
Jean De Lannoy, Service Publications OCDE
avenue du Roi 202, B-1060 BRUXELLES. Tel. 02/538.51.69

BRAZIL – BRÉSIL
Mestre Jou S.A., Rua Guaipa 518,
Caixa Postal 24090, 05089 SAO PAULO 10. Tel. 261.1920
Rua Senador Dantas 19 s/205-6, RIO DE JANEIRO GB.
Tel. 232.07.32

CANADA
Renouf Publishing Company Limited,
61 Sparks Street (Mall), OTTAWA, Ont. KIP 5A6
Tel. (613)238.8985-6
Toll Free: 1-800.267.4164
2182 ouest, rue Ste-Catherine,
MONTRÉAL, Qué. H3H 1M7. Tel. (514)937.3519

DENMARK – DANEMARK
Munksgaard Export and Subscription Service
35, Nørre Søgade
DK 1370 KØBENHAVN K. Tel. +45.1.12.85.70

FINLAND – FINLANDE
Akateeminen Kirjakauppa
Keskuskatu 1, 00100 HELSINKI 10. Tel. 65.11.22

FRANCE
Bureau des Publications de l'OCDE,
2 rue André-Pascal, 75775 PARIS CEDEX 16. Tel. (1) 524.81.67
Principal correspondant :
13602 AIX-EN-PROVENCE : Librairie de l'Université.
Tel. 26.18.08

GERMANY – ALLEMAGNE
OECD Publications and Information Center
4 Simrockstrasse 5300 BONN Tel. (0228) 21.60.45

GREECE – GRÈCE
Librairie Kauffmann, 28 rue du Stade,
ATHÈNES 132. Tel. 322.21.60

HONG-KONG
Government Information Services,
Publications/Sales Section, Baskerville House,
2nd Floor, 22 Ice House Street

ICELAND – ISLANDE
Snaebjörn Jónsson and Co., h.f.,
Hafnarstraeti 4 and 9, P.O.B. 1131, REYKJAVIK.
Tel. 13133/14281/11936

INDIA – INDE
Oxford Book and Stationery Co. :
NEW DELHI-1, Scindia House. Tel. 45896
CALCUTTA 700016, 17 Park Street. Tel. 240832

INDONESIA – INDONÉSIE
PDIN-LIPI, P.O. Box 3065/JKT., JAKARTA, Tel. 583467

IRELAND – IRLANDE
TDC Publishers – Library Suppliers
12 North Frederick Street, DUBLIN 1 Tel. 744835-749677

ITALY – ITALIE
Libreria Commissionaria Sansoni :
Via Lamarmora 45, 50121 FIRENZE. Tel. 579751/584468
Via Bartolini 29, 20155 MILANO. Tel. 365083
Sub-depositari :
Ugo Tassi
Via A. Farnese 28, 00192 ROMA. Tel. 310590
Editrice e Libreria Herder,
Piazza Montecitorio 120, 00186 ROMA. Tel. 6794628
Costantino Ercolano, Via Generale Orsini 46, 80132 NAPOLI. Tel. 405210
Libreria Hoepli, Via Hoepli 5, 20121 MILANO. Tel. 865446
Libreria Scientifica, Dott. Lucio de Biasio "Aeiou"
Via Meravigli 16, 20123 MILANO Tel. 807679
Libreria Zanichelli
Piazza Galvani 1/A, 40124 Bologna Tel. 237389
Libreria Lattes, Via Garibaldi 3, 10122 TORINO. Tel. 519274
La diffusione delle edizioni OCSE è inoltre assicurata dalle migliori librerie nelle
città più importanti.

JAPAN – JAPON
OECD Publications and Information Center,
Landic Akasaka Bldg., 2-3-4 Akasaka,
Minato-ku, TOKYO 107 Tel. 586.2016

KOREA – CORÉE
Pan Korea Book Corporation,
P.O. Box n° 101 Kwangwhamun, SEOUL. Tel. 72.7369

LEBANON – LIBAN
Documenta Scientifica/Redico,
Edison Building, Bliss Street, P.O. Box 5641, BEIRUT.
Tel. 354429 – 344425

MALAYSIA – MALAISIE
University of Malaya Co-operative Bookshop Ltd.
P.O. Box 1127, Jalan Pantai Baru
KUALA LUMPUR. Tel. 51425, 54058, 54361

THE NETHERLANDS – PAYS-BAS
Staatsuitgeverij, Verzendboekhandel,
Chr. Plantijnstraat 1 Postbus 20014
2500 EA S-GRAVENHAGE. Tel. nr. 070.789911
Voor bestellingen: Tel. 070.789208

NEW ZEALAND – NOUVELLE-ZÉLANDE
Publications Section,
Government Printing Office Bookshops:
AUCKLAND: Retail Bookshop: 25 Rutland Street,
Mail Orders: 85 Beach Road, Private Bag C.P.O.
HAMILTON: Retail: Ward Street,
Mail Orders, P.O. Box 857
WELLINGTON: Retail: Mulgrave Street (Head Office),
Cubacade World Trade Centre
Mail Orders: Private Bag
CHRISTCHURCH: Retail: 159 Hereford Street,
Mail Orders: Private Bag
DUNEDIN: Retail: Princes Street
Mail Order: P.O. Box 1104

NORWAY – NORVÈGE
J.G. TANUM A/S
P.O. Box 1177 Sentrum OSLO 1. Tel. (02) 80.12.60

PAKISTAN
Mirza Book Agency, 65 Shahrah Quaid-E-Azam, LAHORE 3.
Tel. 66839

PHILIPPINES
National Book Store, Inc.
Library Services Division, P.O. Box 1934, MANILA.
Tel. Nos. 49.43.06 to 09, 40.53.45, 49.45.12

PORTUGAL
Livraria Portugal, Rua do Carmo 70-74,
1117 LISBOA CODEX. Tel. 360582/3

SINGAPORE – SINGAPOUR
Information Publications Pte Ltd,
Pei-Fu Industrial Building,
24 New Industrial Road N° 02-06
SINGAPORE 1953. Tel. 2831786, 2831798

SPAIN – ESPAGNE
Mundi-Prensa Libros, S.A.
Castelló 37, Apartado 1223, MADRID-1. Tel. 275.46.55
Librería Bosch, Ronda Universidad 11, BARCELONA 7.
Tel. 317.53.08, 317.53.58

SWEDEN – SUÈDE
AB CE Fritzes Kungl Hovbokhandel,
Box 16 356, S 103 27 STH. Regeringsgatan 12,
DS STOCKHOLM. Tel. 08/23.89.00
Subscription Agency/Abonnements:
Wennergren-Williams AB,
Box 13004, S104 25 STOCKHOLM.
Tel. 08/54.12.00

SWITZERLAND – SUISSE
OECD Publications and Information Center
4 Simrockstrasse 5300 BONN (Germany). Tel. (0228) 21.60.45
Local Agents/Agents locaux
Librairie Payot, 6 rue Grenus, 1211 GENÈVE 11. Tel. 022.31.89.50

TAIWAN – FORMOSE
Good Faith Worldwide Int'l Co., Ltd.
9th floor, No. 118, Sec. 2,
Chung Hsiao E. Road
TAIPEI. Tel. 391.7396/391.7397

THAILAND – THAILANDE
Suksit Siam Co., Ltd., 1715 Rama IV Rd,
Samyan, BANGKOK 5. Tel. 2511630

TURKEY – TURQUIE
Kültur Yayinlari Is-Türk Ltd. Sti.
Atatürk Bulvari No : 191/Kat. 21
Kavaklidere/ANKARA. Tel. 17 02 66
Dolmabahce Cad. No : 29
BESIKTAS/ISTANBUL. Tel. 60 71 88

UNITED KINGDOM – ROYAUME-UNI
H.M. Stationery Office,
P.O.B. 276, LONDON SW8 5DT.
(postal orders only)
Telephone orders: (01) 622.3316, or
49 High Holborn, LONDON WC1V 6 HB (personal callers)
Branches at: EDINBURGH, BIRMINGHAM, BRISTOL,
MANCHESTER, BELFAST.

UNITED STATES OF AMERICA – ÉTATS-UNIS
OECD Publications and Information Center, Suite 1207,
1750 Pennsylvania Ave., N.W. WASHINGTON, D.C.20006 – 4582
Tel. (202) 724.1857

VENEZUELA
Libreria del Este, Avda. F. Miranda 52, Edificio Galipan,
CARACAS 106. Tel. 32.23.01/33.26.04/31.58.38

YUGOSLAVIA – YOUGOSLAVIE
Jugoslovenska Knjiga, Knez Mihajlova 2, P.O.B. 36. BEOGRAD.
Tel. 621.992

Les commandes provenant de pays où l'OCDE n'a pas encore désigné de dépositaire peuvent être adressées à :
OCDE, Bureau des Publications, 2, rue André-Pascal, 75775 PARIS CEDEX 16.
Orders and inquiries from countries where sales agents have not yet been appointed may be sent to:
OECD, Publications Office, 2, rue André-Pascal, 75775 PARIS CEDEX 16.

67849-07-1984

OECD PUBLICATIONS, 2, rue André-Pascal, 75775 PARIS CEDEX 16 - No. 43057 1984
PRINTED IN FRANCE
(92 84 04 1) ISBN 92-64-12607-4